REFORMING RETIREMENT POLICIES

A Statement by the Research and
Policy Committee of the Committee for
Economic Development
September 1981

Library of Congress Cataloging in Publication Data

Committee for Economic Development. Research and Policy
    Committee.
    Reforming retirement policies.

    Includes bibliographical references.
    1. Old age pensions—Government policy—United States.
2. Social security—Government policy—United States.
3. Retirement income—Government policy—United States.
I. Title
HD7106.U5C593 1981   331.25′22′0973   81-15207
ISBN 0-87186-773-7 (lib. bdg.)   AACR2
ISBN 0-87186-073-2 (pbk.)

First printing: September 1981
Paperbound: $5.00
Library binding: $6.50
Printed in the United States of America by Pearl Paul Ltd.
Design: Stead, Young & Rowe, Inc.

COMMITTEE FOR ECONOMIC DEVELOPMENT
477 Madison Avenue, New York, N.Y. 10022
1700 K Street, N.W., Washington, D.C. 20006

CONTENTS

REFORMING
RETIREMENT POLICIES

RESPONSIBILITY FOR CED STATEMENTS ON NATIONAL POLICY

The Committee for Economic Development is an independent research and educational organization of two hundred business executives and educators. CED is nonprofit, nonpartisan, and nonpolitical. Its purpose is to propose policies that will help to bring about steady economic growth at high employment and reasonably stable prices, increase productivity and living standards, provide greater and more equal opportunity for every citizen, and improve the quality of life for all. A more complete description of CED is to be found on page 66.

All CED policy recommendations must have the approval of the Research and Policy Committee, trustees whose names are listed on page vii. This Committee is directed under the bylaws to "initiate studies into the principles of business policy and of public policy which will foster the full contribution by industry and commerce to the attainment and maintenance" of the objectives stated above. The bylaws emphasize that "all research is to be thoroughly objective in character, and the approach in each instance is to be from the standpoint of the general welfare and not from that of any special political or economic group." The Committee is aided by a Research Advisory Board of leading social scientists and by a small permanent professional staff.

The Research and Policy Committee is not attempting to pass judgement on any pending specific legislative proposals; its purpose is to urge careful consideration of the objectives set forth in this statement and of the best means of accomplishing those objectives.

Each statement is preceded by extensive discussions, meetings, and exchanges of memoranda. The research is undertaken by a subcommittee, assisted by advisors chosen for their competence in the field under study. The members and advisors of the subcommittee that prepared this statement are listed on page viii.

The full Research and Policy Committee participates in the drafting of findings and recommendations. Likewise, the trustees on the drafting subcommittee vote to approve or disapprove a policy statement, and they share with the Research and Policy Committee the privilege of submitting individual comments for publication, as noted on pages vii and viii and on the appropriate page of the text of the statement.

Except for the members of the Research and Policy Committee and the responsible subcommittee, the recommendations presented herein are not necessarily endorsed by other trustees or by the advisors, contributors, staff members, or others associated with CED.

RESEARCH AND POLICY COMMITTEE

[1]Voted to approve the policy statement but submitted memoranda of comment, reservation, or dissent or wished to be associated with memoranda of others. See page 62.

NOTE/A complete list of CED trustees and honorary trustees appears at the back of the book. Company or institutional associations are included for identification only; the organizations do not share in the responsibility borne by the individuals.

PURPOSE OF THIS STATEMENT

In recent years, the Trustees of the Committee for Economic Development have become increasingly concerned with a number of long-term trends that are weakening the U.S. economy and impairing its ability to compete in world markets. More and more of our research and study program has been turned toward such critical issues as the excessive growth of government expenditures, overregulation, inflation, energy supply, and lack of capital formation. Two of our most important current projects deal with developing industrial strategies to revitalize the economy and developing strategies to improve the productivity of U.S. business and industry.

It is within this overall context of policies to develop a healthy, noninflationary economy that we undertook this study of the nation's public and private retirement systems. When we began this project, we were keenly aware of the human dimensions of the retirement problem. Major changes in retirement policies are needed to avoid imposing of real hardships and insecurity on future retirees and impossible funding burdens on future working generations.

But we were also aware of the enormous impact that retirement systems have on the economy and of the special problems that inflation and slow growth pose for pension systems. Policy makers will soon be faced with crucial decisions on retirement and pension issues. We believe it is vitally important that these decisions reflect the need for a retirement system that not only generates retirement benefits but also contributes to economic growth, helps reduce inflation, and increases capital formation.

This report presents strategies that are critical to achieving a growing, productive economy. For too many years, policy makers have taken a narrow, shortsighted approach to retirement issues, not fully recognizing the impact that retirement decisions have on the economy as a whole or examining the implications that today's retirement decisions have for the decades ahead.

WIDE-RANGING IMPLICATIONS

Achieving noninflationary economic growth will require actions on many fronts. Such problems as low productivity, high inflation, and low capital formation do not exist in isolation—each is linked to the other and to many of the other problems that affect the economy. It is important to recognize these interrelationships when making decisions on retirement issues.

For example, long-term economic growth and stability depend on adequate capital for investment. Because of the huge amount of money involved in both public and private pension systems, this nation needs a balanced and economically sound public and private retirement system that can provide an important part of the capital needed for long-term investment.

In addition, increased productivity will require the most effective use of human as well as investment resources. And national decisions on retirement policy will have a strong impact on how long workers remain in the productive labor force.

Tax and regulatory policies that encourage—rather than discourage—saving, investment, and growth will be essential to rebuilding the economy. We believe that the tax measures and incentives outlined in this statement will not only provide adequate financing for retirement systems but will also contribute to increased capital formation and saving for productive growth.

THE NEED FOR ACTION

Throughout this statement, as in many other recent CED reports, we stress the need for a long-term, comprehensive view. This is especially important to decisions on retirement policy because action is needed now in order to avoid the possibility of serious social and economic disruptions in the next century. No action, action delayed, or too little action will not only place increased burdens on both workers and retirees but will also reduce the possibility that the retirement system can become a positive force for future economic growth.

But this does not need to happen. If work begins now, we believe that Social Security, increased personal savings incentives, and private pensions can develop into workable, affordable, and humane policies while at the same time helping the economy to grow and produce more for all to enjoy.

SPECIAL CONTRIBUTIONS

The Subcommittee that prepared this report included a number of Trustees and advisors with extensive expertise and experience in pension and retirement issues. A list of Subcommittee members and advisors appears on page viii.

We are especially indebted to the chairman of the Subcommittee, William C. Greenough, Trustee of TIAA-CREF, for his skillful and persuasive leadership. Special recognition is also due Dan M. McGill, chairman of the Department of Insurance at the Wharton School of the University of Pennsylvania, who served as project director; Kenneth McLennan, CED's vice president and director of industrial studies, who served as staff counselor; and Claudia P. Feurey, CED's Director of Information, who served as project editor, for their incisive approach to this critical issue.

We are also deeply grateful to the John D. and Catherine T. MacArthur Foundation for its support of this project.

Franklin A. Lindsay
Chairman
Research and Policy Committee

CHAPTER ONE

INTRODUCTION AND SUMMARY OF RECOMMENDATIONS

Over the last forty-five years, the United States has built a huge and diversified assortment of pension and retirement programs designed to provide a decent standard of retirement living for American workers and their dependents. Efforts to attain this goal have too often been uncoordinated and shortsighted and have failed to recognize that changes in some retirement programs affect the growth of personal saving as a source of retirement income as well as the overall performance of the economy. Consequently, unless changes are made, this nation faces a future in which the cumulative effects of all these retirement policy decisions could prove disastrous. Yet, with the proper changes, the United States can evolve retirement policies that society can afford, that satisfy the diverse needs of the elderly, and that support a healthy and expanding economy.

Progress in extending retirement benefits for the elderly has been substantial. Throughout the 1960s and 1970s, the proportion of the elderly living in poverty, as measured by cash income, declined from about 35 percent to 14 percent, which is only slightly higher than the percentage for the entire population.[1]

Improvement in the income security of the elderly has resulted from the rapid economic growth that occurred during the 1960s, the expansion of

---

[1] / June A. O'Neill, "Sources of Income of the Elderly, With Special Reference to Elderly Women," Working Paper (Washington, D.C.: Urban Institute, 1981).

private pensions, and the growth of federal expenditure programs for the elderly, including higher Social Security benefits and the expansion of in-kind benefits such as Medicare and food stamps. In fact, when in-kind benefits are included in elderly income, poverty among the elderly falls below the incidence for the rest of the population.[2] But if public and private retirement systems continue to promise more improvements, especially in benefits during periods of economic slowdown, there is strong reason to believe that neither government nor business will be able to ensure that these new obligations will be met.

By late 1982, low productivity, persistent unemployment, and high inflation will cause a financing crisis for the Social Security system, which will have insufficient funds to meet mandated retirement benefits. Congress can be expected to take action to solve the immediate financing problem, but such a solution would only be temporary. Demographic projections indicate that by the early part of the next century, almost one in five Americans will be over 65 years of age, compared with one in ten in the mid-1960s, when government programs for the elderly were expanded. *These basic trends suggest that a retirement disaster is on the way early in the twenty-first century. Action is needed now to avert it because Social Security is widely regarded as a long-term commitment that cannot be easily changed.*

Social Security is not the only part of the retirement system that is in trouble. Employer pension plans for federal employees have extremely large unfunded liabilities, and the cost to the federal budget of meeting benefit payments is exceptionally high given the relatively small number of workers covered by these plans. The finances of state and local governments are being strained by the rapidly increasing share of expenditures they must allocate to pension fund payments. In contrast, the vast majority of private pension plans will generally have less difficulty meeting their obligations to future retirees because larger portions of their liabilities are funded.

In the past decade, policy makers in Congress and successive Administrations and at the state and local government levels have failed to recognize the full implications of their policies concerning retirement income for the elderly. Public policy for retirement cannot be developed in a vacuum; rather, it must be made in the context of all programs affecting retirement income, with full recognition of the need for a growing role for private pensions and personal savings. In the private sector, business executives, labor leaders, and various interest groups have sometimes failed to understand

---

[2] The Business Roundtable, *Statement of the Retirement Income Policy Positions of The Business Roundtable* (Washington, D.C.: The Business Roundtable, 1981), p. 1.

the potential impact of their retirement policy decisions on the future employment of workers, as well as on the economic health of their particular industries and the overall economy.

We believe that unless basic changes are begun now in the way this nation views retirement income and in the public and private systems that provide it, future working generations will bear impossible funding burdens, and future retirees will face insecurity and hardship. But we also believe that if the role of private-employer pensions and personal saving is expanded, this nation can develop a retirement system that not only cares adequately for its retirees but also can be a positive force for noninflationary economic growth.

THREE CRITICAL FORCES

AN AGING AMERICA

At the turn of this century, only 4 percent of the U.S. population was over the age of 65. Today, this group accounts for 11 percent of the population, and the proportion is expected to double in the next fifty years.

Longer life expectancy has resulted in a higher percentage of the population reaching the normal retirement age of 65. And more people are living and collecting retirement benefits *well* beyond 65. In 1900, 29 percent of the elderly population was over 75. By 1970, that proportion had risen to 39 percent. By the year 2000, it is expected to be 43 percent.

Concurrent with this increase in the number of retired workers has been a steady drop in the birthrate. The birthrate is significantly lower at present than it was in the 1960s and well below the 2.1 children per family needed to sustain the present population level.

The combination of increased longevity and a low birthrate means that when the large postwar "baby boom" generation begins retiring in the year 2010, there will be proportionately fewer workers financing the retirement benefits of a larger elderly population.

At the present time, there are 30 Social Security beneficiaries for every 100 workers. By 2025, under optimistic economic and demographic assumptions (increased birthrate and very rapid economic growth), there will be about 44 beneficiaries per 100 workers. Under more pessimistic assumptions (continuation of present birthrates and 2 to 3 percent annual growth in real gross national product), there will be 65 Social Security beneficiaries for every 100 workers by the year 2025.[3]

---

[3]/ Social Security Administration, *1981 Social Security Trustees Report* (Washington, D.C.: U.S. Government Printing Office, 1981).

Assuming no significant increase in the labor force participation rate of the elderly, the dependency ratio of the aged to the active labor force could more than double by the year 2025. Even a decline in the dependency ratio of young age groups would fail to permanently offset this dramatic increase in the proportion of nonworkers to workers.

These trends foreshadow an increasingly heavy retirement burden on the decreasing proportion of workers who will have to produce the resources from which retirement income is drawn. For example, if no changes are made in the Social Security program, the tax rate needed to finance benefits fifty years from now will be more than double the current rate of 13.30 percent of payroll (6.65 percent of current wages and salary paid by the employer and 6.65 percent paid by the employee).[4] Such increases in the Social Security payroll tax would reduce individuals' real disposable income and their ability to save, thus inhibiting the expansion of funds available for the investment needed to stimulate economic growth.

INFLATION

Retired people used to be the forgotten victims of inflation. Now, Social Security and other federal retirement systems provide benefit adjustments that in some ways overcompensate because they include increases in costs, such as home prices and associated financing costs, that do not generally affect older people. There is a serious question about whether younger workers, who are not so protected, have an obligation to fully protect retired federal employees and Social Security recipients from the ravages of inflation. During the past decade, while the real income of the elderly was rising, the real aftertax income for the median family (one full-time employed wage earner with two children) declined from $8,412 in 1970 to its present level of about $8,000 (measured in 1972 dollars).[5]

On the other hand, because benefits from most private pensions are fixed at retirement, inflation has severely reduced the real income retirees receive from private pension plans. Prices rose by an average of 7.4 percent a year during this last decade. At this rate—"modest" by today's standards—the purchasing power of the private pensions received by workers who retired ten years ago has already been reduced more than 50 percent. Although many corporations have provided ad hoc increases in benefits to help compensate for inflation, they find it increasingly difficult to predict their pension obligations during periods of uncertainty caused by inflation.

---

[4] Social Security Administration, *1980 Social Security Trustees Report* (Washington, D.C.: U.S. Government Printing Office, 1980).

---

[5] Tax Foundation, *Monthly Tax Features* 24, no. 8 (September 1980): 1.

INCREASED CONCERN WITH SOCIAL EQUITY

Income security policies for the elderly have produced significant benefit improvements but have also resulted in certain inequities. Large increases in the Social Security benefit levels mean that those who have retired or who are retiring now are receiving much more out of the system than they put in. The reverse may be true for those retiring thirty years from now.

Complex problems of equity also arise from the fact that government policies protect a major share of the income of the elderly against inflation but that most of those paying for these benefits have no such complete and automatic protection. Despite improvements in retirement policies, there are still some coverage gaps in both private and public plans. Moreover, among some groups, such as elderly women, the incidence of poverty is still unacceptably high.

A HEAVY BURDEN

During the last forty years, this nation has made a commitment to bringing America from a country that provided little protection for its elderly to a country that provides a wide variety of both public and private forms of assistance. Until now, Social Security has generally been able to adjust to changing social and economic conditions. Congress was able to increase Social Security benefits by gradually raising taxes over a period of economic growth and by bringing into the system workers previously excluded.

But if the cost of retirement programs continues to escalate at the present rate, there will be serious economic consequences for most groups in society. Between 1950 and 1977, private and public contributions (including Social Security costs) to retirement income programs increased from 2.3 percent of GNP to 8.2 percent;[6] with additional scheduled increases in Social Security taxes, this percentage will rise even higher. The future obligations of private pension plans are not a burden on future generations when the plans are fully funded. In contrast, the growth of Social Security is unfunded, and future obligations depend on contributions from future generations of workers. *It is inconceivable that this nation will deliberately choose to place such a burden on future generations or that future generations will, in fact, stand for it. There must be a more equitable balance between the benefits from retirement policies and the responsibility for providing these benefits.*

---

[6] President's Commission on Pension Policy, *Coming of Age: Toward a National Retirement Policy* (Washington, D.C.: U.S. Government Printing Office, 1981), p. 11.

A BETTER BALANCE

What is needed is a comprehensive examination of all U.S. retirement programs, as well as the role of private saving, in light of long-term social, demographic, and economic trends. Many of the problems of retirement programs are the result of a number of well-intentioned pension and benefit actions aimed at immediate needs and desires without corresponding attention to costs and long-term consequences. This has been especially true of policies affecting Social Security and public-employer pension plans.

Public policy makers should first recognize that retirement policies have significant implications for such problems as inflation, unemployment, lagging productivity, and reduced competitiveness. Moreover, the vast amounts of money required to finance public pension payments have, on balance, inhibited capital formation, thereby reducing investment in the productive base of the economy. Once the economic impact of retirement policies is fully understood, the nation can take steps to restore a reasonable balance between pension benefits and other economic needs.

A NEW STRATEGY FOR RETIREMENT POLICY

The goal of the new strategy should be the forging of policies that will assure a minimum level of retirement income for all workers and their families and at the same time provide an environment in which individuals, both workers and employers, have the opportunity and the responsibility to meet their own retirement income goals above this minimum level of income.

The primary goal that we are recommending in this policy statement will not be easily achieved. **The enactment of general policies that will promote a healthy, growing, productive, and noninflationary economy are prerequisites for achieving this goal.** The United States must break the current vicious circle of low saving, low productivity, and high inflation. No specific reforms will succeed in solving the retirement problem without a more effective overall national commitment to greater productivity, increased saving, and noninflationary economic growth. Only a growing economy can allow the nation to increase real benefits for retired workers and correct the inequities and inadequacies in retirement policies.*

We recommend the development of a broad-based, diversified retirement system, supported by a healthy economy and, in turn, supporting the productive growth of that economy. This policy statement recommends measures to achieve this goal. Chapter 2 briefly describes the current environment in which retirement policies must be reformed. Later in the statement, we make specific recommendations for reforming Social Security

---

*See memorandum by ROBERT R. NATHAN, page 62.

(Chapter 3), encouraging private pensions (Chapter 4), and developing incentives for increased personal saving (Chapter 5). A summary of these recommendations begins on page 8.

We recommend a retirement policy strategy that encourages individuals to acquire their retirement income from three complementary tiers.

- **Social Security** is the first tier. Social Security should provide a basic floor of retirement income for virtually all working members of society and their dependents. Defining what constitutes a basic floor is a difficult task. In order to continue to provide such a level of support for future generations, a number of important changes are required, including gradually raising the normal retirement age, revising the indexing formula, and revising the tax status of Social Security taxes and benefits.

- **Employer pensions** provide the second tier. Although most workers can expect some form of employer pension, policies should be developed to improve funding, broaden coverage, and increase the contribution of private pension funds to capital formation.

- **Personal savings** form the third tier. Not enough emphasis has been placed on encouraging personal saving and investment to provide a significant part of retirement income. Indeed, many tax regulations have actually discouraged personal saving. We call for a number of policy changes to make saving for retirement an attractive and achievable goal.

These three elements should be the focus of a strategy for achieving a balanced retirement policy. In addition, we urge policy makers to recognize that working beyond the traditional retirement age can be a desirable and important source of income for some of the elderly. Retirement policy should not discourage workers from acquiring income from this source.

It is inevitable that there will also be some people who, through a variety of circumstances, will not have enough retirement income to sustain even a subsistence level of living. Although policy should be designed to make this group as small as possible, those elderly who are unfortunate enough to fall into it should be cared for through welfare programs. However, this income-support system should be clearly distinguished from Social Security.

In addition to enhancing the financial soundness of the retirement system and expanding access to pension coverage, the steps we recommend will have broad positive effects on the economy as a whole. For example, if actions are taken to restrict the growth of Social Security, overall disposable income will be increased. With the proper tax policies to provide incentives for personal saving, this increased disposable income can be attracted to investment in new private plant and equipment, a prerequisite for improving productivity and assuring real economic growth.

In addition, by gradually raising the normal retirement age, the nation can lighten the financing burden on the working population and at the same time achieve the desirable social goal of providing older Americans with an opportunity to contribute to the economy. Such actions could also help increase total real GNP sufficiently to raise the average real disposable income for both workers and retirees.

If efforts begin now, Social Security, employer pensions, and individual savings can be developed into workable and affordable sources of retirement income and at the same time aid in the real growth of the economy, producing more goods and services for all to enjoy.

SUMMARY OF MAJOR RECOMMENDATIONS

This Committee's major recommendations advocate a three-tiered approach to retirement income based on Social Security, employer pensions, and personal savings.

• **Social Security** should provide a basic floor of retirement income upon which an individual can build. We make the following recommendations:

—The normal retirement age for Social Security should be gradually raised to 68 and the early retirement age to 65 in steps that produce no abrupt change in the benefits of anyone about to retire.* This change should begin as soon as possible, with the retirement age increasing two months a year until the higher retirement age is reached by about the year 2000.** (It would, of course, also be possible to retain the current early retirement age of 62 years if Social Security benefits for those retiring before the normal retirement age were gradually lowered to reflect the longer period over which they would receive benefits and the reduced number of years in which they would contribute to the system.) This proposal is one of the most important of our recommendations for both the short-run and the long-run control of the escalating costs of the Social Security system brought about by the increasing proportion of elderly in the population. It is based on the fact that retired workers are living significantly longer and are generally in better health than their counterparts in previous decades.

---

*See memorandum by J. W. McSWINEY, page 62.

**See memorandum by RAPHAEL CARRION, JR., page 62.

—So that both workers and retirees will be treated fairly, increases in Social Security benefits should be linked to an appropriate price index or to the rise in average pretax wages of workers if that should turn out to rise less than the price index. For this purpose, the government should develop a supplemental price index that reflects the consumption patterns of the elderly more accurately than the currently used Consumer Price Index (CPI) does. Policy makers should review past trends in Social Security benefits and wages and consider some adjustment of benefit levels, such as indexing at less than 100 percent for a period of several years, to partially correct for past increases in Social Security benefits in excess of increases in average wage rates.*

—Employee contributions to Social Security should be excluded from current taxable income; instead, the benefits paid to the individual after retirement should be included as part of his or her taxable income at that time. This should be accomplished on a phased-in basis and should be consistent with the need for overall budget discipline. If, and only if, these changes are made, it would be feasible to eliminate the retirement earnings test for all Social Security retirees and thereby provide a greater incentive to continue working.

—Given public policies that will encourage greater individual saving and broader coverage under private-employer pensions, the Social Security "replacement ratio" (the ratio of a person's initial Social Security benefits to his or her earnings level prior to retirement) should not be increased further; indeed, as the other recommendations in this statement are implemented, it should gradually decline to a lower level.

—Any attempt to solve Social Security financing problems should reject general revenue financing as a solution.**

—All early retirement benefits under government retirement systems (Social Security and government-employer plans) should gradually be reduced actuarially from normal retirement age benefits to fully recognize the benefits that will be paid out during an average early retiree's lifetime. Retirement systems should not be used to provide severance pay, retraining, relocation allowances, hazardous-duty premiums, or other personnel benefits different from the need for income following retirement at the normal age.

—Federal workers and other noncovered workers should be brought into the Social Security system. As a compromise, if necessary, at least all new government employees should be brought into the Social Security system beginning now.***

*See memorandum by JOHN F. WELCH, JR., page 63.

**See memorandum by ROBERT R. NATHAN, page 63.

***See memorandum by JOHN H. FILER, page 63.

• **Employer pensions** can be improved and their coverage expanded through a number of tax and regulatory actions.

—A government mandate for private-employer pensions is neither necessary nor feasible. Nevertheless, changes in the tax law would make it more attractive for more employers to establish pension plans.

—Employee contributions to both private and government pension plans should be tax-deductible, and pension benefits should be included in taxable income when received. This will encourage the growth of employer pension plans in all industries, thereby enlarging this channel for saving and investment.

—Employers should have maximum flexibility in setting their own pension and retirement policies. They should be able to raise, gradually and voluntarily, the normal retirement ages in their pension plans, consistent with whatever changes are made in the Social Security retirement age. This and the preceding proposal will encourage more workers and employers to contribute to employer pension plans that can be tailored to the specific needs of their industrial and occupational structures.

—To encourage greater portability of vested pension benefits, an employee leaving an employer is now allowed to continue in that employer's plan and ultimately to receive retirement benefits from it. As an alternative, the employer could be permitted to offer the employee leaving the pension plan the option of transferring vested benefits into an individual retirement account (IRA) or life insurance annuity. This may be an especially attractive option when the pension plan is fully funded. Where the plan is not fully funded, a difficult problem exists with respect to providing equal treatment for those leaving and those remaining in the plan. All cash withdrawals of over $500 should be forbidden.*

—The federal government should take action to require all public-employer pension plans to accurately report their unfunded liabilities, as well as their normal total annual cost, to the general public in a manner similar to the Financial Accounting Standards Board's requirement that private-employer plans accurately report unfunded liabilities.

• **Personal savings** as a source of retirement income have been greatly neglected. In fact, a number of public policies have actually discouraged saving and investment.

---

*See memoranda by THOMAS B. McCABE and by J. W. McSWINEY, page 64.

—The current maximum annual tax-deductible contributions permitted under personal retirement plans (Keogh Plans and IRAs) should be raised substantially.

—The recently enacted Economic Recovery Tax Act contains saving provisions that are similar to this Committee's recommendations for expanding the role of personal savings as a source of retirement income. We therefore endorse this legislation and urge that on the basis of experience, the additional personal saving incentives that we recommend be considered in the future.

—The appropriate goal for the combined total of tax-deductible annual contributions into all such individual and corporate retirement plans on behalf of any one individual should ultimately move much closer to the maximum currently allowed for a person under a corporate pension plan. We recognize that these liberalized limits will have to be phased in gradually in order to allow future changes in them to take account of saver response and of their effect on federal tax revenues. As an interim goal, IRA and Keogh limits could be raised to the level to which they would have risen if they had been adjusted in the same way that defined-contribution pension plan levels have been adjusted under the Employee Retirement Income Security Act of 1974, commonly known as ERISA. In the future, such flexible adjustment of maximum contribution levels should be applied to IRAs and Keoghs as well as to corporate defined-contribution plans.

—Businesses that already have pension plans should be encouraged to integrate some measure of individual saving into their benefit packages voluntarily through such measures as matching thrift programs, profit sharing, and voluntary employee contributions.*

• Suitable employment opportunities for capable elderly individuals are needed if the maximum advantages of the higher-retirement-age provisions are to be realized. Changes in job design and work schedules will be needed to take into account the capabilities and interests of older workers. Public policy should remove any existing regulations and labor market practices that inhibit flexibility in work arrangements for older workers.

• Even a work-related retirement system as comprehensive as the one we are recommending may not succeed in coping with the retirement income needs of *all* citizens. For a variety of reasons, some elderly in-

---

*See memorandum by FRAZAR B. WILDE, page 64.

dividuals will probably continue to receive inadequate income. The most effective way to assist this small proportion of the elderly is to rely on a supplemental system of targeted welfare-type payments, rather than to enrich Social Security benefits for everyone.

● Our comprehensive recommendations for strengthening the U.S. retirement system will produce additional savings that can finance increased investment in plant and equipment. In this way, pension plans and personal savings will make an increased contribution to the economic growth that is essential to a sound retirement system in the future.*

*See memoranda by ROBERT R. NATHAN, page 62 and by JOHN SAGAN, page 64.

CHAPTER TWO

PENSIONS AND THE POLICY ENVIRONMENT

In 1960, only about 8 percent of the population was 65 years of age or older. The elderly now represent about 11 percent of all Americans, and by the early part of the next century, this group could constitute approximately 20 percent of the population.

Figure 1 shows that if the current birthrate and level of immigration continue on their present trends, the proportion of workers to retirees will decline sharply. The significance of the continuation of the current birthrate of about 1.8 children per family and increased life expectancy is revealed in Figure 2. If there is no change in the birthrate, over one of every five Americans could be 65 or older by 2030. This represents an elderly dependency rate twice as great as that in the mid-1960s, when government programs for the elderly were expanded.[1] A major medical advance resulting in increased longevity could further alter these projections and their detrimental consequences for providing retirement income.

Unless changes are made in programs for older Americans, the projected absolute and proportionate increases in the number of elderly will place an increasingly severe burden on the federal budget. Since 1960, fed-

---

[1] The increase in the elderly dependency ratio will be partially offset by a decline in the dependency ratio of children.

14

eral expenditures for the elderly have risen from 13 percent to approximately 24 percent of the budget,[2] with higher Social Security benefit levels accounting for much of this increase.

The improvements in the economic position of the elderly in the past decade occurred at a time when the average real earnings of workers declined.[3] The maximum level of Social Security has more than quadrupled, and the tax rate rose substantially during the 1970s. In addition, higher Social Security taxes and insufficient reliance on employer pensions and individual savings have had an adverse effect on capital accumulation. This has

[2]/ June A. O'Neill, "Sources of Income of the Elderly, With Special Reference to Elderly Women," Working Paper (Washington, D.C.: Urban Institute, 1981), p. 1.

[3]/ The real average weekly earnings of nonagricultural private-sector employees declined from $103 in 1970 to $95 in 1980 (measured in 1967 dollars). U.S. Department of Commerce, Bureau of the Census, *Statistical Abstract of the United States* (Washington, D.C.: U.S. Government Printing Office, 1980), p. 421.

FIGURE 1

Estimates and Projections of Annual Population Change, 1940–2025

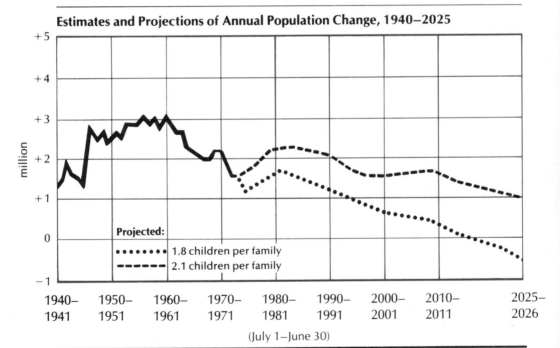

SOURCE: Presented at U.S. Congressional Research Service Seminar, "Changing Demographics and Implications for Public Policy," May 1980. Derived from U.S. Bureau of the Census data. Estimates assume current levels of legal and illegal immigration will remain constant.

contributed to a low rate of investment in plant and equipment and has made it difficult to achieve a high rate of productivity improvement. Unless current productivity trends are reversed, we believe that neither the elderly nor the rest of the population will be able to maintain their present standard of living.*

DEVELOPMENT OF THE U.S. PENSION SYSTEM

Social Security was established in 1935 to ensure that the bulk of the working population would have a minimum degree of financial security in old age. The program was designed to serve as a "floor of protection" that would have to be supplemented by other resources if the retired person was to enjoy a more comfortable standard of living.

The system is still funded as it was originally, on a pay-as-you-go basis, with tax payments made by current workers and employers going almost immediately to the retired population. Other aspects of the system, however, have changed dramatically, most notably the level and scope of benefits.

The original Social Security Act provided only old-age benefits for individual workers. In 1939, survivor and dependent benefits were added. From 1939 to the 1950s, some adjustments were made, but Social Security generally provided fairly low benefits and was sustained by a low level of

FIGURE 2

Percent of the Total Population in the Older Age Groups, 1900–2040

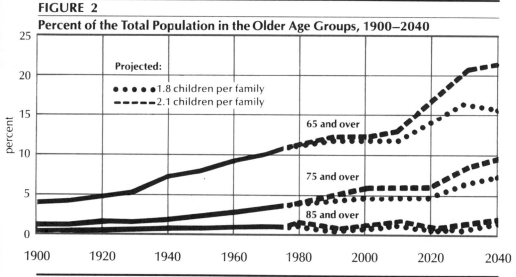

SOURCE: Presented at U.S. Congressional Research Service Seminar on *Changing Demographics and Implications for Public Policy,* May 1980. Derived from U.S. Bureau of the Census data that assume annual legal immigration of 400,000.

*See memorandum by ROBERT R. NATHAN, page 62.

taxes. In the 1950s, the growth of Social Security accelerated as more and more workers were brought into the system. In the early 1950s, self-employed workers were brought under the program, and workers in the nonprofit sector were given the choice of joining; and in 1954, state and local employees were given a similar option. Full benefits for workers who become disabled, regardless of age, were added in 1956. In 1965, Medicare benefits were enacted.

Social Security benefit levels were raised ten times between 1950 and 1972. By far the most extensive changes occurred in 1972, when Congress, in addition to broadening a wide range of benefits, provided for automatic increases in benefits tied to rises in the CPI.

In 1980, Social Security contributions were collected from approximately 115 million workers and their employers. Benefits under the Old Age Survivors and Disability Insurance part of the system of $117.1 billion were paid to approximately 35 million people, including retired and disabled people, their dependents, widows and widowers, and children of deceased workers. In real dollars, this represents a 186 percent increase over the benefits paid in fiscal 1970.[4]

Benefits vary with work history, covered earnings, and marital status. For example, a couple each over age 65 with the wage earner retiring in January 1982 will receive $12,227 a year if their earnings record reflects the maximum taxable wages. A couple retiring in similar circumstances but having earned only the federal minimum wage will receive $6,395. A couple whose earnings are in the middle will receive $9,637. These relatively high benefits have led many to believe that Social Security has achieved its goal of minimum income adequacy for workers and may, indeed, have surpassed it.

On average, the elderly population has substantially improved its retirement income position. But there continue to be special and often severe problems for workers who have not had a lifelong history of work and for some divorced and widowed dependents. In elderly families headed by a white male, the incidence of poverty in 1977 was 6.2 percent, only half the incidence for the overall population. However, for white women in unrelated units (living alone or with nonrelatives), the poverty incidence was 25.8 percent; and for black women, it was 60.7 percent.[5] The data in Table 1 indicate that Social Security benefits as a source of retirement income are

---

[4]/ U.S. General Accounting Office, *What Can be Done to Check the Growth of Federal Entitlement and Indexed Spending*, Report to the Congress of the United States (Washington, D.C.: U.S. Government Printing Office, 1981), attachment.

---

[5]/ O'Neill, "Sources of Income for the Elderly, With Special Reference to Elderly Women," p. 6.

TABLE 1

**Receipt of Income and Share of Income for Aged Families
and Unrelated Individuals, by Source, 1977**

	Percent of Elderly Receiving Income from Specific Source	Mean Amount Received (dollars)[a]	Relative Importance of Specific Income Source (percent of total income)
Families with head 65 years old and over			
Earnings	48.2	9,016	34.8
Social Security	92.5	4,439	32.9
Public assistance	2.3	1,484	0.3
Supplemental Security Income	8.4	1,456	1.0
Other transfers	10.3	1,933	1.6
Asset income	65.6	3,096	16.3
Employee pensions and other[b]	39.7	4,140	13.2
Total			**100.0[c]**
Unrelated individuals 65 years old and over			
Earnings	17.4	3,828	12.5
Social Security	92.6	2,687	46.7
Public assistance	1.7	1,026	0.3
Supplemental Security Income	12.5	1,090	2.6
Other transfers	7.0	1,417	1.9
Asset income	55.9	2,066	21.7
Employee pensions and other[b]	26.1	2,927	14.3
Total			**100.0**

[a]The mean income from all sources was $12,482 for families with members 65 years and older and $5,326 for unrelated individuals 65 and older.

[b]Includes private- and government-employer pensions, alimony, annuities, and other forms of periodic payments.

[c]Percent total has been rounded to nearest whole number.

SOURCE: U.S. Department of Commerce, Bureau of the Census, *Characteristics of the Population Below the Poverty Level, 1977* (Washington, D.C.: U.S. Government Printing Office, March 1979), Table 38.

of particular significance for the elderly living in unrelated units. A greater proportion of these individuals are women. A serious problem exists because some of the elderly have insufficient work experience or have lost their dependency status, which normally provides Social Security coverage, and therefore are not covered by the system.

EMPLOYER PLANS

Until World War II, private pension plans were rare; in 1929, for example, there were only 397 such plans in existence. During World War II, the federal tax code was changed to clarify the tax position of pensions; and in the Inland Steel case decision of 1948, the National Labor Relations Board ruled that retirement pensions were a form of wages and therefore subject to compulsory collective bargaining under the Taft-Hartley Act. In the 1950s, the push for private pension coverage accelerated rapidly.

With the rapid growth of private pensions came new problems. Some plans were poorly administered, and there were a few well-publicized cases of misuse of pension fund assets. In addition, in the 1960s, many plans were underfunded. In response to these problems, in 1974 Congress enacted ERISA. This complex law established standards for the protection of benefit rights, disclosure, funding, fiduciary responsibilities, and administration and created the Pension Benefit Guaranty Corporation to insure plans in the event of failure.

The growth of employer pensions is impressive. Figure 3 shows that the proportion of full-time workers in the private nonagricultural sector between 25 and 64 years of age participating in employer pension plans has risen from less than 50 percent in 1957 to more than 75 percent in 1979. It should be noted that this growth has occurred in both corporate plans and plans designed to encourage small employers to establish retirement arrangements for themselves and their employees. For example, Keogh Plans and IRAs now cover about 5 percent of the labor force.[6]

These data show that the vast majority of workers who are full-time members of the labor force and who have completed the period of high labor mobility experienced in the career path of young workers now participate in an employer pension plan. In addition, some 40 percent of this group of full-time workers now have vested rights in such pension plans, and this proportion is growing rapidly.

---

[6]/ Sylvester J. Schieber and Patricia George, *Retirement Income Opportunities in an Aging America, Coverage and Benefit Entitlement* (Washington, D.C.: Employee Benefit Research Institute, forthcoming 1981), p. V18.

FIGURE 3

Private Pension Plan Rates of Participation, Vesting, and Benefit Receipt for Private-Sector Nonagricultural Full-Time Workers between 25 and 64 Years of Age[a]

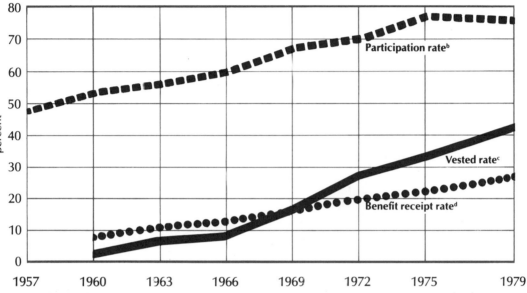

^aThis employment base was calculated as follows: (Nonagricultural workers on full-time schedules minus full-time federal, state, and local workers) multiplied by percent of full-time workers between 25 and 64 years of age.

^bParticipation refers to proportion of employees who have satisfied the requirements of a private-sector employer pension plan and are participating in such a plan.

^cVesting refers to employees who have a nonforfeitable right to a private-sector employer pension plan.

^dBenefit receipt rate is the number of employees receiving retirement benefits under a private-sector employer plan as a percent of participants.

SOURCES: Data for nonagricultural workers on full-time schedules and the percentage of workers between 25 and 64 are taken from U.S. Department of Labor, Bureau of Labor Statistics, *The Handbook of Labor Statistics* (Washington, D.C.: U.S. Government Printing Office), December 1980 for 1969–1979, Table 23, p. 54, and December 1972 for 1959–1968, Table 22, p. 67. Data on federal, state, and local employees are taken from the *Economic Report of the President* (Washington, D.C.: U.S. Government Printing Office, January 1981), Table B-35, p. 273. From unpublished data received from the Bureau of Labor Statistics, it was estimated that approximately 11 percent of government employees are part-time workers; therefore, the data from the *Economic Report* have been reduced by 11 percent. These estimates also assume that the age distribution for government workers is similar to that of the rest of the nonagricultural full-time work force.

Data on participation, vesting, and benefits are from Sylvester J. Schieber and Patricia George, *Retirement Income Opportunities in an Aging America, Coverage and Benefit Entitlement* (Washington, D.C.: Employee Benefit Research Institute, forthcoming, 1981), Tables III-1, III-6, and III-7.

Table 2 compares the average annual labor force growth rate with the growth rates for participation, vesting, and pension benefit receipt. As employer pension plans have matured, the rates of growth for vesting and benefit receipt have far outstripped the labor force growth in every five-year period over the past two decades. The growth rate of participation has exceeded the rate of growth in the labor force in all periods except the past five years, during which labor force growth was especially rapid. These findings demonstrate that a very high proportion of full-time workers can look forward to vested pension rights and the eventual receipt of retirement income from private-sector employer pensions.

Despite the growth of participation in employer pension plans, the full potential of such plans is far from realized. Public policy should be concerned about the 25 percent of full-time workers who do not participate in employer pension plans. Many employers, especially small employers, have no formal retirement plan, and the costs to small employers are such that it is difficult for them to start new plans. Public policy has done little to encourage small employers and their employees to develop individual saving plans for workers' retirement. Indeed, with the enactment of ERISA, the government temporarily reduced the incentives, especially for small employers, to establish private pensions. Before ERISA, the net number of new private plans being created each year increased consistently; the annual av-

TABLE 2

Average Annual Rate of Growth of Employment of Private-Sector Wage and Salary Workers and Rate of Growth of Participation, Vesting, and Benefit Receipt of Employer Pension Plans (percent)

Period	Nonagricultural Full Time Civilian Workers: Ages 25–64 Employment	Participation	Vesting	Benefit Receipt
1960–1969	1.2	3.7	17.7	9.9
1970–1974	1.2	3.8	12.5	7.7
1975–1979	4.2	3.3	10.3	7.9

SOURCE: Adapted from Figure 3.

erage between 1972 and 1974 was 51,967 new plans. This dropped significantly between 1975 and 1977 (after ERISA) to an average of 15,009, with only 3,494 new plans created in 1977. However, since 1978, the rate of creation of new plans has increased, especially for defined-contribution plans.[7]

If private-employer pension plans are to play an even more important role in providing retirement income for the elderly, incentives must be provided for employers to establish pension plans as well as for employees to contribute to them. If this is done, there will be a significant opportunity for achieving increased private-employer pension coverage not only for full-time workers but also for part-time employees. Such incentives, however, must permit employers and their employees to design pension plans that are consistent with the economic environment and needs of their firms.

POTENTIAL PROBLEMS IN MEETING FUTURE RETIREMENT OBLIGATIONS

As recently as ten years ago, policy makers and the public were not concerned about the fundamental soundness of public and private retirement programs. Social Security benefits were broadening, but the rate at which the taxes that supported these increases were rising was not disturbing. Well-managed and well-funded private pension plans could easily be expected to predict and supply the funds needed to meet their obligations. Many public-employer plans, especially at the federal level, were seriously underfunded but were described as "actuarially sound" because of the presumed ability of government to continue to increase taxes.

However, as we noted in Chapter 1, a number of economic forces and social trends have greatly diminished the ability of both public and some private systems to deliver what they have promised. The belief of younger workers that they can expect to retire on secure and adequate pensions is being severely shaken. A recent survey indicates that 73 percent of those between the ages of 25 and 44 have little or no faith that funds will be available to pay their Social Security benefits.[8]

The double threat of continuing inflation and the certainty of more and older retirees and relatively fewer contributing workers is straining both the public and some private systems. These strains, combined with demands

---

[7] Based on Internal Revenue Service data on establishment of tax-qualified pension plans as quoted in Schieber and George, *Retirement Income Opportunities in an Aging America, Coverage and Benefit Entitlement.*

---

[8] Based on a public opinion survey by Peter Hart, Inc., and reported in the *Daily Report for Executives* by the Bureau of National Affairs, May 15, 1981, p. G-5.

for more, wider, and larger benefits, are creating what could become an untenable situation for retirement plans.

The cost of meeting the future obligations of the Social Security system is staggering. In 1977, Congress was forced to pass the largest tax increase of any kind in U.S. history to finance the next ten years of Social Security needs. In 1981, employer and employee each pay 6.65 percent of an employee's salary up to a maximum wage of $29,700. That tax bite is scheduled to rise to 7.15 percent each for employer and employee in 1986 on a maximum projected wage base of $46,200.[9] According to the Social Security Administration's own estimates, combined tax rates in 2050 could be 25 percent of covered payroll or, if economic productivity growth is modest and demographic developments are unfavorable, as high as 45 percent.[10]

Inflation creates problems for retirees receiving benefits. In most private plans, the monthly benefit is fixed at retirement; consequently, retired employees are generally faced with a decline in the purchasing power of their pensions. Inflation is a much less serious problem for the financial soundness of the plan. Investment earnings tend to increase as inflation progresses, and these increases can be used to help increase pensions being paid or to meet the added cost of defined-benefit plans based on final salary. But in periods of rapidly rising inflation, increased investment earnings tend to lag behind the inflation rate.

Lack of real income growth in the 1970s has also made it more difficult for people to make any substantial contribution to their retirement income in the form of savings. They have less real disposable income during periods of inflation; in addition, "bracket creep" occurs as the tax base for individuals rises and they move into higher tax brackets. This process increases the average tax rate for all individuals and reduces their ability to save.[11]

Unless changes are made now, the increasingly heavy burden imposed on workers and companies by the Social Security system could cause major economic and social distortions. If more and more resources are diverted from the productive economy in order to maintain or continue to increase real Social Security benefits, productivity improvement will con-

---

[9] Based on Social Security Administration, *1981 Social Security Trustees Report* (Washington, D.C.: U.S. Government Printing Office, 1981).

[10] Social Security Administration, *1980 Social Security Trustees Report* (Washington, D.C.: U.S. Government Printing Office, 1981), and information from the Health Care Financing Administration.

[11] Michael J. Boskin, Mark Gertler, and Charles Taylor, *The Impact of Inflation on U.S. Productivity and International Competitiveness* (Washington, D.C.: National Planning Association, 1980), p. 19.

tinue to remain low, inflation could become more intractable, and economic growth could be significantly slowed.

Adverse economic conditions have created a serious short-term financing problem for the system. But even if we deal successfully with this immediate problem, it is important to realize that the Social Security system also has basic *long-term* problems that are best solved with *long-lead-time* solutions. Action must begin now if an even more serious crisis is to be avoided twenty or thirty years hence.

We recommend that private and public policy makers take the specific policy actions now that are needed to increase the roles of employer pensions and personal savings in providing retirement income while reducing the relative role of Social Security. Such policy actions will require some reform of the Social Security component of our diverse retirement system and *simultaneous* policy changes to provide incentives for personal saving for retirement and to encourage the growth of employer plans, especially for small employers, who constitute an increasing source of new employment opportunities.

THE ESSENTIAL FOUNDATION: A GROWING ECONOMY

Whatever actions are taken, the future health of public and private pension systems is linked directly to the future health of the economy. *Noninflationary growth is a necessary foundation on which to build a system of adequate and affordable retirement benefits.*

The Committee for Economic Development (CED) has in recent years published several policy statements that address these issues. The most recent, *Fighting Inflation and Rebuilding a Sound Economy* (1980), proposed a variety of coordinated strategies to control inflation and stimulate growth. We continue to urge the adoption of recommendations contained in that statement and emphasize that the central aim of economic policy should be a progressive, year-by-year reduction in the rate of inflation until essential price stability is achieved. Retirement policies that encourage capital formation and saving can directly contribute to such an anti-inflationary strategy.

WHAT GOAL FOR RETIREMENT?

There is currently much debate over what constitutes an adequate income for an individual retiring after a normal working life. Some have suggested that retiring workers should, through a combination of Social Security, employer pensions, and personal savings, be able to sustain a standard of living equal to the standard they had achieved, in terms of disposable income, just before retirement. This is generally the highest standard of living enjoyed by people during their working years. Others suggest that an appropriate level would be one equivalent to the average standard of living of the working population and would recognize the fact that the elderly generally do not have to support dependent children.

There are problems in trying to develop a standard national goal for retirement income. American workers and their families are too diverse and their needs too varied to be covered by a uniform standard. Many workers may wish to or may have to scale down their living standards after retirement. Others may wish to sacrifice more during their working lives in order to enjoy more in later years. Accordingly, flexibility rather than rigidity should be a major feature of any U.S. retirement system.

The government has an obligation to assure all citizens a minimum income based on demonstrated need. Public policy has developed a welfare system to provide such protection for those who do not reach that income level through Social Security and other means.

For retired workers with a sufficient lifetime earnings history, and for their dependents, Social Security properly represents a basic level of earnings-related benefits that is above the minimum income level under the welfare system. However, even a work-related retirement system of Social Security, employer pensions, and personal savings may not succeed in coping with the retirement income needs of *all* citizens. For a variety of reasons, some elderly individuals will probably still receive an income below the minimum income level that the government has an obligation to assure for its citizens. The most effective way to assist this small proportion of the elderly is to rely on a supplemental system of targeted welfare-type payments, rather than to enrich Social Security payments for everyone.

Social Security should not be regarded as the sole source of income for retirees. As shown in Table 1, the elderly as a group acquire a substantial proportion of their income from assets and various forms of retirement plans. Public policy should create an environment in which individuals can have both the choice of, and the responsibility for, determining the level of their own retirement income.

THREE TIERS OF PROTECTION

Government should not establish a specific, rigid definition of what percentage of preretirement income is desirable in retirement or what standard of living should be achieved by all workers. The government should, however, create and maintain economic and social policies that make it possible for an individual, through a variety of means, to achieve his or her desired standard of living in retirement. Although we are firmly committed to maintaining the Social Security system, we believe that each American should have as much flexibility as possible in planning and providing for retirement.

If government adopts policies that will restrain the future growth of Social Security, promote the growth of employer pension plans, and encourage greater personal saving and investment, this nation will be able both to afford and to supply a decent retirement for all its citizens.

A retirement policy should promote a diversified and balanced three-tiered approach for individuals to acquire retirement income. The first tier should be provided by Social Security. Social Security is an important source of earnings-related income benefits for most retirees. However, a diversified retirement system should also encourage saving, which can be transferred into the investment necessary for economic growth. In order for the nation to benefit from this approach to retirement policy, the relative role of Social Security should not be permitted to expand. This requires increasing recognition that in the early years of retirement, up to about 70 years of age, many of the elderly can, and will wish to, increase their retirement income through earnings.

The recommendations presented in Chapter 3 will, we believe, go a long way toward restoring the financial health of the Social Security system and toward easing the burden on the working population and the economy. These changes can be made gradually and without inflicting hardships on the retired population.

The second tier of the retirement system should be provided by employer pensions. For many workers, an employer pension combined with Social Security provides a comfortable, sometimes generous, retirement. In Chapter 4, we recommend policies that would encourage wider coverage and provide employees and employers with incentives to develop pension plans that meet the diverse needs of all sectors of the economy. However, an improvement in the general economic environment, including a reduction in inflation, would do much to stimulate the growth of the private pension system.

The third tier should be made up of personal savings. Not enough attention is paid to the importance of personal saving and investment both for future retirement income and for building up the nation's capital resources. It is through their personal saving decisions that individuals achieve the greatest flexibility in adjusting the shape and timing of their lifelong consumption patterns. If the growth of Social Security is to be restricted, accumulated personal savings will have to become an increasingly important component of retirement income. Top priority must be given to encouraging a higher level of personal saving.

Government and employers should place no regulatory or other unnecessary barriers in the way of those workers who wish to continue in employment after age 65. More flexible work patterns—changing work assignments; tapering off both in work and in earnings; part-time, temporary, and seasonal work; flexible hours; retraining—can be rewarding both for employers and for older workers. This Committee examined such alternatives in detail in its policy statement *Jobs for the Hard-to-Employ: New Directions for a Public-Private Partnership* (1978).

CHAPTER THREE

NEW CHALLENGES FOR SOCIAL SECURITY

In the nearly fifty years since its founding, Social Security has become the most important source of income for most elderly Americans. Virtually all people over 65 are now eligible for benefits. For 56 percent of elderly couples and 73 percent of single people receiving benefits, Social Security checks account for more than half their total income.

In spite of its current financing problems, the Social Security program has historically been efficiently managed and has had the nearly universal support of workers, employers, and policy makers. Improved benefits have played a major role in the dramatic turnaround in the income of the elderly, and essentially all American workers now have some protection against loss of income because of retirement, disability, or death.

Social Security's traditional political and social strength has rested on low tax rates and the widespread belief that today's payments assure tomorrow's benefits. However, in recent years, it has become apparent that the system, which has functioned so smoothly for so long, is in serious financial trouble. Fully indexed to the CPI, benefits are rising at a rate that many would argue outstrips even the real rate of inflation. Demographic trends show that as the "baby boom" generation retires, there will be a vast increase in the number of retired nonworkers to be supported by a decreasing proportion of workers. In 1960, there were 20 Social Security beneficiaries for every 100 workers contributing to the system; by 1980, the ratio had risen to 31 beneficiaries per 100 contributing workers. This ratio is expected to rise to a range of 40 to 70 by the middle of the next century.[1]

Faced with this problem, Congress enacted stiff new tax increases to take effect between 1979 and 1990. But these increases have already proved insufficient to carry the system in the immediate future, and they will not cover rising costs for the entire seventy-five-year period used in the long-term estimates for Social Security planning. Even with the scheduled large tax increases, experts believe that revenues will again fall short early in the next century.

Using its intermediate estimates, the Social Security Administration predicts that under the current structure, combined employer and employee tax rates will need to rise to 16.6 percent of payroll in 2010 and 25.4 percent in 2030. According to a recent pessimistic projection (based on slower economic growth, lower fertility rates, and more substantial reductions in mortality rates), the combined Social Security tax could reach 21.4 percent, 36.3 percent, and 45.3 percent in 2010, 2030, and 2050 respectively.[2]

Even those tax increases that have already been passed will put a significant strain on the economy. They will reduce both consumer purchasing power and the ability of individuals to save.[3] In addition, higher Social Security taxes levied on employers tend to increase the prices of goods and services, reduce employee wages and the hiring of new workers, and restrict the availability of funds for new investment.

Clearly, Social Security is entering a new era. The combined forces of inflation, slow economic growth, and demographic change, as well as the

[1] Social Security Administration and Health Care Financing Administration, *Summary of the 1981 Annual Reports of the Social Security Boards of Trustees* (Washington, D.C.: U.S. Government Printing Office, July 6, 1981), p. 14. Beneficiaries are all persons receiving Social Security benefits, including surviving spouses, the disabled, and dependents, in addition to retired persons.

[2] As projected by the Health Care Financing Administration for the *1980 Social Security Trustees Report.*

[3] Although consumption in specific income groups may fall, aggregate consumption may increase as tax revenues are transferred from persons with lower propensities to consume to those with higher propensities.

maturing of the system itself, have brought about this financial crisis. The challenge that policy makers face is how to reshape the system so that the costs to the working generation are kept manageable and yet still fulfill the social and economic goal of providing basic benefits to retirees.

WHAT IS THE APPROPRIATE LEVEL FOR SOCIAL SECURITY BENEFITS?

In recent years, objectives for retirement income have frequently been expressed in terms of proportion of disposable income before and after retirement. If low-income retirees receive about 80 percent of their preretirement income and high-income workers receive about 60 percent, they will usually be able to maintain their preretirement standard of living.

Such a retirement income goal is very generous. For most people, it means a standard of living throughout their retirement years that is substantially higher than they enjoyed when they were younger and raising a family. Such a large diversion of income from earlier years or transfer payments from current workers through Social Security should not be mandated. Any retirement income goals chosen should include income from all sources—in-kind and other welfare benefits, Social Security, employer pensions, personal savings, and any other sources. A preretirement standard of living as a retirement income goal is not appropriate if it is to be financed only through Social Security. It is important to note that a very large proportion of this high objective is already provided by such benefits.

Under current law, from Social Security alone, a worker who retires at age 65 with average covered earnings will receive tax-free benefits equal to about 40 percent of his or her gross earnings immediately before retirement. If the worker is married to a nonworking spouse over 65, there will be an additional 20 percent, for a total of 60 percent replacement of earnings. Individuals whose lifetime earnings are in the lowest range qualify for benefits of about 60 percent of final earnings and may get an additional 30 percent for a nonworking spouse, for a total of 90 percent. An average worker with very high earnings, equal to the current taxable earnings base, will be eligible for a benefit of about 28 percent of earnings, increasing to 42 percent if he or she has an eligible nonworking spouse.

Over the years, the Social Security Administration has studied the actual replacement rates received by its beneficiaries. A recent study of men and women who began collecting benefits in 1975 revealed that for all workers, the average replacement rate was 50 percent and that fewer than 5 percent of workers had a replacement rate lower than 40 percent. For the lowest-income workers, the benefit often exceeded 100 percent replacement. If benefits at age 65 were payable to a retired worker and dependent spouse, the combined replacement rate (in constant dollars) in almost all cases was 70 percent or more.[4]

The current retirement benefit levels under Social Security are sufficient to ensure a basic level of retirement income for most people. **Given public policies that will encourage both broader coverage under employer pensions and a higher level of individual savings, the Social Security replacement ratio should not increase further. Indeed, as the other recommendations in this statement are implemented, it should gradually decline to a lower level.[5]**

If no changes in the system are made, and even if overall benefits are simply maintained, rather than raised, Social Security will continue to cost more and more. But we believe that there are alternatives to continuing to raise taxes (which are eventually paid by workers) and the rate base on which taxes are levied without imposing undue hardships on the retired population or undue burdens on this country's workers.

NEW TAX TREATMENT FOR SOCIAL SECURITY

Throughout the history of taxation of retirement systems in this country, with minor exceptions, employee contributions have been made out of aftertax income, and the benefits resulting from employee contributions have not been included in taxable income. This has been true for both private pension plans and Social Security.[6] The result of this is that a young couple trying to raise a family, buy a house, and meet other expenses from the lower salaries usually available to younger workers is also transferring a substantial amount of income to retired people and is paying tax on the amount transferred. In contrast, the retired person does not have to include the Social Security benefits in taxable income. It is time that employee contributions to Social Security and to all retirement plans, public and private, within reasonable limits, be made from pretax income and that the benefits resulting from such employee contributions be included in taxable income.

---

[4] Social Security Administration, Orlo R. Nichols, *Actuarial Notes* (Washington, D.C.: U.S. Government Printing Office, July 1979). For this study, replacement rates were computed on four different earnings bases: earnings for the years 1951 to 1974, indexed according to average wages; highest five years of earnings during the period, unindexed; last five years of earnings, indexed according to average wages; and highest ten years of earnings, indexed according to the CPI.

[5] Several approaches to reducing the replacement ratio deserve consideration. For example, the *initial* Social Security benefit is calculated on the basis of a wage index. Subsequent benefits are based on a price index. A congressional advisory panel has recently recommended that the replacement ratio would have been lower if *initial* benefits had been based on a price index.

---

[6] For private-sector employer plans, this has resulted in almost complete elimination of employee contributions to the plans except in part of the nonprofit private sector, where employee contributions need not be included in taxable income. See Chapter 4 for a discussion of employer pension plans.

CED recommends that all employee contributions to Social Security, to regular employer retirement programs, and to other saving plans dedicated to retirement be excluded from current taxable income. We concurrently recommend that the benefits from all such sources be included in taxable income when received. This should be accomplished on a gradual, phased-in basis to avoid inequities and to be consistent with maintenance of an appropriate degree of overall budget discipline.* Study should begin now on ways to accomplish this new tax treatment of Social Security and how to phase in the change so that both current workers and retirees are fairly treated.

Including retirement benefits received in taxable income does not mean that those elderly relying on small pensions or basic Social Security benefits would necessarily pay taxes on these benefits. Double exemptions for those over age 65 and the regular exclusions mean that most of these retirees would not be in taxable income brackets. But middle-income and well-to-do people who have been receiving tax-free transfer benefits would have to include them in income after a phase-in period or grandfather provision.

If this new treatment of Social Security taxes and benefits were to be enacted, it would, of course, result in a deferral of revenue to the Treasury. If employee contributions to Social Security taxes were tax-deferred, there would be an initial annual revenue loss of $25 billion.[7] It must also be recognized that the taxes paid by retirees on their Social Security benefits could not make up this difference because most retirees are in much lower tax brackets than the working population and the double exemption for people over 65 would also shelter much of their benefit income. The revenue loss that would accompany this change could be phased in so that it would be absorbed as part of plans to reduce the overall level of taxation while retaining an appropriate degree of fiscal discipline.

If excluding Social Security contributions from taxable income and including the benefits in taxable income when received were to become public policy, this Committee would then, and only then, endorse the elimination of the Social Security retirement earnings test, which limits the amount a retiree can earn and still receive Social Security benefits. The retirement earnings test was designed to avoid taxing one group of workers in order to transfer part of their earnings to another group of workers who happen to be over age 65 or otherwise eligible for retirement benefits.** The idea is that benefits are to be paid only upon withdrawal of an eligible person from the

---

[7] President's Commission on Pension Policy, *Coming of Age: Toward a National Retirement Income Policy* (Washington, D.C.: U.S. Government Printing Office, 1981), p. 55.

---

*See memorandum by JOHN F. WELCH, JR., page 63.

**See memorandum by THOMAS B. McCABE, page 65.

work force. But if Social Security benefits were to be included in taxable income subject to the progressive income tax, this could serve as a suitable substitute for the test.

REVISING INDEXING

Since 1975, Social Security benefit payments have been automatically adjusted each year to reflect the full increase in the general CPI for urban wage earners and clerical workers. Because of the rapid upsurge in inflation, this automatic indexing has imposed very large costs on the Social Security system. It is estimated that the 14.3 percent cost-of-living adjustment established in July 1980 added nearly $17 billion to Social Security outlays in fiscal 1981 alone. [8] The most recent adjustment of 11.2 percent will continue to push Social Security costs up. Adjustment costs will escalate in future years as the level of benefits continues to increase and as further benefit adjustments are calculated from a higher base.

These massive cost increases have led to widespread calls for a basic reexamination of full and automatic indexation of Social Security benefits. There is growing agreement that such indexation arrangements add to the spiraling of inflation and can thus become at least partially self-defeating. Moreover, it is widely believed that the CPI, as currently computed, has serious shortcomings as a measure of inflation and of the *impact* of inflation on retirees. Finally, there are significant questions about whether the present indexation arrangement is fair to other groups in American society in view of the fact that, at least during the recent past, retirees have had more protection against inflation than members of the active work force have had.

We share these concerns and urge that the Administration and Congress take early action to improve the present procedures for determining cost-of-living adjustments for Social Security recipients. In deciding how this might best be accomplished, however, it is important to distinguish among a number of separate issues that are involved in the debate over the indexation of Social Security benefits: whether Social Security should be given *any* form of protection against the effects of inflation, how automatic such adjustments should be, what statistical measures should be used to calculate the degree of inflation, and whether the adjustments should be partial or complete.

---

[8] / Executive Office of the President, *Report on Indexing Federal Programs* (Washington, D.C.: U.S. Government Printing Office, January 1981), p. 14.

DISCRETIONARY VERSUS AUTOMATIC ADJUSTMENTS

The present system of fully automatic adjustments was introduced in the early 1970s in the belief that it would "depoliticize" the process of making inflation adjustments and thereby prevent excessive benefit increases. It was also argued that automatic adjustment would prevent overly erratic changes in the pattern of increases and facilitate better long-term planning by Social Security recipients.

However, after nearly six years, it has become clear that automatic indexing to the CPI has some serious disadvantages. It leaves no room for flexible adjustments to unusual and unforeseen developments, such as the significantly larger increases in the CPI than in average remuneration of workers that occurred in the 1974–1975 and 1979–1980 periods. Since 1972, Social Security benefits have gone up substantially because of exceptionally large increases in benefit levels and the indexing of the benefits to the CPI, including a number of years during which benefits were double-indexed.[9] In real terms, since 1969, average dollar benefits have risen 70 percent more than the CPI.[10] In effect, the combination of inflation and low productivity growth led to a decline in workers' real purchasing power during these periods while Social Security benefits remained fully or overly protected.

AN APPROPRIATE INDEX

There are strong indications that the index used to calculate inflation adjustments under Social Security has significantly overstated the general rise in the cost of living in recent years, both because of the way in which home ownership costs are calculated and because the index is based on

---

[9] Double indexing occurred because of the way automatic indexing was implemented under the 1972 Social Security amendments. Under these amendments, any automatic adjustment resulted in an increase in the entire schedule of benefits for both those receiving Social Security benefits and those currently contributing to the system. This was designed to maintain the future Social Security replacement rate of those not currently receiving benefits. However, those still working received an additional adjustment to their future Social Security benefit level because their salary in current dollars was also raised, and raised substantially in a period of rapid inflation.

The effect of the 1972 amendments was to provide those working and contributing to the Social Security system with a substantial increase in their future replacement rate because they had a "double" adjustment for inflation. After several years, this problem was recognized and remedied in the 1977 amendments through the "decoupling" provisions.

---

[10] Executive Office of the President, *Report on Indexing Federal Programs*, p. 7.

fixed, outdated (1972–1973) consumption patterns of urban workers. The upward bias of the index appears to have been particularly pronounced during the recent period of very sharp increases in prices and mortgage interest rates.

The use of a modified index in calculating inflation adjustments for Social Security benefits has been suggested as a more accurate reflection of spending patterns. For example, the adjustments could be based on a CPI that substitutes a rental equivalent for the present method of computing the housing component. Such a measure is already being published by the Bureau of Labor Statistics on an experimental basis. It has been estimated that if the rental equivalent had been used over the past four years, the overall rise in the CPI for the period would have been reduced by over 5 percentage points and would have resulted in a substantial savings in Social Security benefit outlays. In a period of falling inflation rates, the effect of using the rental equivalent is uncertain but could be in the opposite direction.

It has also been suggested that an index based directly on the spending patterns of older persons would show a slower rate of price increases than the general CPI, which is geared to the entire population. Over 70 percent of the housing units headed by an elderly person are owner-occupied, and it is estimated that more than three-quarters of such homeowners have no outstanding mortgage.[11] Consequently, Social Security beneficiaries as a group are overcompensated for an increase in housing prices as measured by the CPI, and this overcompensation is even greater in a period of rapid inflation. On the other hand, there may be other components of the CPI for which the outlays of the elderly rise more rapidly than the increase in the CPI. Clearly, it is desirable to adjust Social Security benefits by using a more accurate index based on more frequent estimates of the consumption patterns of the elderly. However, the construction of such an index may require a substantial survey of consumer spending.

THE DESIRABLE EXTENT OF INDEXATION

Should inflation adjustments for Social Security beneficiaries compensate for all, or only a part of, the inflation that has taken place? A persuasive case can be made for the view that the effects of inflation should be equitably shared by the entire population and that no one segment of the population should be fully protected from inflation at the expense of other segments.

---

[11]/ Sylvester J. Schieber and Patricia George, *Retirement Income Opportunities in an Aging America, Coverage and Benefit Entitlement* (Washington, D.C.: Employee Benefit Research Institute, forthcoming 1981), p. 14-14a.

So long as Social Security benefits represent a floor of minimum income protection for their recipients, there is justification for protecting that minimum from too much erosion because of inflation, even though it must be admitted that such protection adds impetus to an inflationary spiral. But the current provisions for inflation indexing of Social Security go too far.

Many of the problems connected with the present indexation system can be alleviated through statistical improvements in the overall CPI and, eventually, through the development of a specialized CPI for older persons. Some improvements should occur in the next few years once the Bureau of Labor Statistics completes the development of a continuous survey of consumer expenditures that will permit regular updating of the market basket on which the CPI is based.

The present system of indexing Social Security benefits to the general CPI as it is currently computed should be changed. **We recommend that as soon as feasible, benefit payments should be tied to a price index that more accurately reflects consumption patterns of older Americans. We urge that strong efforts be made to develop such an index within a reasonable period of time and that adequate funding be made available for this purpose. Pending construction of a specified index for older persons, Social Security cost-of-living adjustments should be based on a modified version of the CPI or on an alternative index that is less subject to upward biases.**

In addition, Social Security indexing needs to recognize that in some circumstances, inflation can actually lead to net reductions in the average standard of living of our society. This has happened in the past several years, for example, as a result of the sharp increases in oil prices charged by the members of the Organization of Petroleum Exporting Countries and of actual declines in productivity. Such a reduction in the standard of living should be shared by all groups. If the price index is rising much more rapidly than average wages, however, the present automatic increase in Social Security benefits will enable the elderly to avoid the decline in real income being experienced by the workers who are currently paying for Social Security benefits. That, we think, is unwise and unfair. **We recommend that in years when the annual average wage of workers rises less than the annual increase in the price index, the annual automatic increase in Social Security benefits should be at the same rate as the rise in average wages.***

Policy makers should consider making some adjustment to Social Security benefits to compensate for the past inequity of fully protecting Social Security beneficiaries while many of those workers financing benefits experienced a decline in real income. Since 1965, the CPI has increased 162 percent, whereas average money wages (Social Security Covered Earnings Series) increased 170 percent. During the same period, Social Security ben-

---

*See memorandum by ROBERT A. BECK, page 65.

efits rose 210 percent, outstripping the rise in both CPI and average wages. Indeed, since 1972, Social Security benefits increased 20 percent in *real terms*, whereas average real wages actually declined 0.6 percent.[12] **We urge policy makers to review past trends in Social Security benefits and wages and to consider some adjustment of benefit levels, such as indexing at less than 100 percent for a period of several years, to partially reflect the past differential between average wage rate changes and increases in Social Security benefits.**

These proposals for determining the automatic increase in Social Security benefits will provide beneficiaries with substantial protection against the inroads of inflation and at the same time ensure that benefit increases do not outstrip improvements in the income of those workers supporting the system.

RETIREMENT AGE

When formulating the Social Security Act, Congress picked age 65 as the normal retirement age and later added 62 as the age for early retirement at reduced benefits. In studying models of retirement programs, the original policy makers looked at public-assistance programs for the aged with age requirements ranging from 65 to 70. For example, the U.S. Railroad Retirement Program, passed by Congress in 1934, used 65. Among the foreign models, both Germany and Britain have used 65.

Retirement at age 65 has remained the norm, although life expectancy and the general health of the elderly have improved substantially in the last forty-five years. As life expectancies continue to rise beyond the norm of fifteen years in retirement, questions arise with regard to whether the retirement age should be adjusted, especially in light of the fact that the "young old" (those between the ages of 62 and 68) are in better health than ever before. There is also the question of whether public policy should encourage all workers to leave the work force and face twenty or more years out of the productive mainstream.

Any policy change that raises the early and normal retirement ages under Social Security in effect removes the present attractive alternative of early retirement for the vast majority of workers. This may be viewed as unfortunate, but there is no other feasible way that future generations of workers can support the prospective level of early and normal age Social Security benefits for the increasing elderly dependency group. Restricting the option of early retirement can produce opportunities for older workers

---

[12]/ David Koitz, "Indexing of Social Security," in Senate Budget Committee, *Indexation of Federal Programs* (Washington, D.C.: U.S. Government Printing Office, May 1981).

as well as net benefits for the rest of society. For many, the economic and social benefits of remaining an active participant in the economy can be substantial. However, a reversal of the trend toward early retirement could reduce the opportunity for upward mobility among younger members of the labor force.

Because the current birthrate is running below the population-replacement rate, those workers who must support the Social Security system in the future will bear a heavy financial burden. Moreover, without an increase in the labor force participation rate of those over 65, the rate of growth in the labor supply twenty years from now may decline.

For these reasons, but especially in light of the need to prevent additional increases in scheduled Social Security taxes, **we recommend gradually raising the normal retirement age to 68 and the early retirement age to 65, to be accomplished by approximately the year 2000.*** This could be done by raising both the normal and the early retirement ages by two months each year from now until the target ages are reached by about the year 2000. (There is, of course, much less need to set a specific early retirement age if the benefits paid prior to the normal retirement age are actuarially reduced. This would require gradually lowering benefits for anyone retiring before age 68. The actuarial reduction would reflect the longer time early retirees are, on average, expected to collect benefits and the fewer years they would contribute to the system, compared with those who retire at age 68.)

This simple, gradual change would help bring the costs and benefits of Social Security in line without causing significant disruption to workers, families, or firms. Raising the normal retirement age is a reversal of the traditional trend toward earlier retirement, but it is important to note that government also has an obligation to the working population that funds Social Security benefits. Unless changes are made in the normal retirement age and early retirement benefits are actuarially reduced, the nation will face the possibility of having to raise taxes to unacceptably high levels or cut benefits drastically. The gradual phase-in would provide ample time for those who would be affected to plan accordingly for their future retirement. *Such a change would not only avoid the short-term Social Security financing crisis, it would also eliminate the projected long-term deficit in the old-age portion of Social Security.*

However, any such change must be made with the recognition that not *all* workers will be able to continue full-time, physically demanding work until these later retirement ages. Public and private pension plans and personnel policies should be designed to reflect the need for employees in particular occupations to move to less demanding types of work and modified

---

*See memorandum by RAPHAEL CARRION, JR., page 62.

work schedules. In addition, public policy should remove any existing regulations and labor market practices that limit flexibility in work arrangements for older workers.

UNIVERSAL SOCIAL SECURITY COVERAGE

The original Social Security Act excluded all state, local, and federal employees and employees of certain nonprofit organizations. Later legislation allowed state and local governments and nonprofit organizations to enter the system voluntarily but excluded civilian federal workers.

The fact that so many government workers, including those who manage the system and influence its future, are not subject to the Social Security tax undermines public confidence in the equity of the system.

If all government employees were brought into the system, it would not only mean greater immediate tax revenues but would also solve the "windfall benefit" problem, whereby a large number of federal workers hold second jobs in the private sector long enough to qualify for disproportionately large Social Security benefits on top of their generous civil service pensions. In 1980, more than half a million civil service beneficiaries drew Social Security in addition to their government pensions. Because the Social Security benefit schedule is designed to favor those with low earnings histories (and all who meet the minimum eligibility requirements receive full medical benefits), those civil service retirees who qualify for minimum benefits are receiving benefits from the system that are far larger than the taxes they contributed to it.

Government workers will come to agree that it is in the national interest for *all* workers to share the responsibility of supporting Social Security. **We recommend that federal employees and other noncovered workers be brought into the Social Security system as soon as possible. As a compromise, if necessary, at least all new government workers and those entering uncovered occupations should be brought into the system beginning now.***

BENEFITS FOR WOMEN

Although Social Security does not pay benefits on the basis of gender, it does base benefits on attachment to the work force and on marital status. The rapid increase in the proportion of women in the labor force, their longer and more permanent attachment to the labor force, changes in family structure caused by the increased divorce rate, and the substantial increase in the proportion of women among the aged population since World War II are focusing attention on a number of issues in a system that was designed when men were the primary wage earners, when families were fairly stable, and when men and women were more equally represented among the elderly.

---

*See memorandum by JOHN H. FILER, page 63.

Under current Social Security law, a one-earner couple receives 150 percent of the basic pension while both are living, and the survivor receives 100 percent after the death of the spouse. Older divorced women (meeting the length of the marriage test of ten years) receive 50 percent of the living ex-spouse's benefit. The spouse benefit has created perceived issues of equity when the benefits of two-earner couples are compared with those of one-earner couples.

Because many women's attachment to the work force has not been continual and has been at lower wages, the spouse benefit resulting from the husband's work record (one-half of his benefit) is frequently larger than the working wife would receive from her own past earnings. This leads to the criticism by some that two-earner couples receive no extra return for the contributions made to the system during the working years by the spouse with the lower lifetime earnings.

It is important to note that women as a group receive more benefits per Social Security tax dollar than men. As the labor force participation rate of women rises and the current male and female earnings differential narrows, some of the perceived inequities in the Social Security treatment of women will become less important because more women will receive benefits directly related to their own earnings. However, in any retirement system that involves an element of "social adequacy," perceived inequities will always remain.

DISABILITY BENEFITS

The financial needs of a family whose primary wage earner becomes totally disabled are as great as, or greater than, those of one whose wage earner has retired. In recognition of this, Social Security provides benefits in the event of total disability, regardless of age. The number of beneficiaries (including dependents) increased sevenfold from 0.7 to 4.9 million between 1960 and 1977.[13] Social Security disability benefits now represent an annual expenditure of almost $17 billion.

Disability has always been difficult to define, and unfortunately, disability income programs are subject to abuse, especially in times of economic downturn. To alleviate the potential for abuse, most experts agree that benefit payments from all sources should not exceed 60 percent of gross earnings before retirement.

Social Security disability payments to a person with eligible dependents often exceed 60 percent of predisability gross earnings, and workers compensation benefits may bring the total to 80 percent. An employer-

---

[13]/ Philip K. Robins and Hoi S. Wai, "Disability Programs and Work Effort: Issues and Products," *Journal of the Institute for Socioeconomic Studies* 6, no. 2 (Summer 1981): 3.

sponsored long-term disability income plan can offset Social Security disability payments by reducing the amount paid from the private-employer disability plan. This reduces the financial incentive for claiming disability and abusing the private plan. However, if an employer wishes to provide the same scale of benefits from a qualified *pension* plan, there are serious limitations on the extent of offsets that may be applied against government disability benefits. This could result in a person having a combined income from a private pension and a government disability program that is higher than predisability gross income. Consequently, unless larger offsets are permitted under a qualified pension plan, it is unattractive for employers to design their pension plans for disability as well as retirement purposes.

GENERAL REVENUE FUNDING

It has been suggested that the Social Security system should be partly financed by the use of general revenues raised by income and corporate taxes. Some proposals would require general revenues to pay for a certain percentage of Social Security. Others would provide general financing for certain benefit programs such as Medicare. Still others would use general revenues to cover the costs of benefits for low-income people.

General revenue financing would merely shift the burden of the Social Security program from payroll taxes to other taxes. Indeed, if Social Security were financed this way, costs could increase because Congress would not be subject to the discipline of having to raise taxes each time benefits were raised. We believe that one of the continued sources of the Social Security system's strength is its payroll tax base. Because current workers expect to join the roll of beneficiaries, a financial base that relates contributions somewhat to benefits plays a large part in assuring beneficiaries that their basic expectations will not be disturbed.

The 1975 Social Security Advisory Council stated that "the [Social Security] deficit can and should be dealt with through the conventional system of earmarked payroll contributions." The council observed that general revenue sources would obscure the cost-benefit relationship and the link between contributions and benefits, would increase unreasonable benefit demands, and could lead to reduced public acceptance of the contributory social insurance program.[14] We conclude that any attempt to solve Social Security financing problems should reject general revenue financing as a solution.

---

[14]/U.S., Congress, House, *Reports of the Quadrennial Advisory Council on Social Security,* H. Doc. No. 94-75, 94th Cong., 1st sess., 10 March 1975, p. 61. The Advisory Council did support general revenue financing of the hospital insurance fund if necessary.

CHAPTER FOUR

THE ROLE OF EMPLOYER-SPONSORED PENSIONS

Three-quarters of full-time nonagricultural private-sector employees between the ages of 25 and 65 are now participating in employer pension plans, and about 40 percent have vested rights to benefits from such plans. In 1977, employers paid $36 billion into pension plans out of the total of $42 billion contributed.[1] Nationally, 1979 private-plan assets had a market value of approximately $375 billion. Estimates prepared for the Department of Labor show that by 1995, assets of private pensions will have risen to almost $3 trillion.[2]

More attention should be paid to expanding the role of private pensions so that they can be a stronger second tier of retirement support for more Americans. During the 1960s and 1970s, the rapid expansion of Social Security benefit levels and costs tended to overshadow the rapid growth of private pensions. Because advance-funded private pension plans contribute to capital formation and provide workers with a source of retirement income, it is in the national interest to create a policy and tax environment in which private plans can continue to expand.

---

[1]/ U.S. Department of Labor preliminary estimate.

---

[2]/ "Analysis of Pension Plan Cost," prepared for Department of Labor by ICS, Inc., July 1980.

THE NATURE OF EMPLOYER PLANS

Most private-sector plans fall into one of two categories: *defined-benefit plans* or *defined-contribution plans*.

Defined-benefit plans are by far the more common, especially in the large-employer and public-plan categories. Federal-employee plans and most state and local public plans, single-employer plans, and multiemployer pension systems provide defined benefits. Under these plans, the benefits a worker will receive at retirement are based on final-average salary, career-average salary, or a flat amount per year of credited service. Final-average-salary plans provide substantial protection against inflation that occurs prior to retirement. Many employers also increase benefits after retirement on an ad hoc basis. Under multiemployer arrangements, a number of employers, usually along with unions in a single trade or economic sector, establish a single plan for all their workers. Under ERISA, companies have the obligation to increase the level of funding of these plans gradually; but in a period of high inflation, projections of future needs can be difficult, and the potential for underfunding is very real.

In a defined-contribution plan, the sponsor does not promise a fixed set of benefits but instead commits itself to contribute to the plan on a stipulated basis on behalf of each plan participant. An individual account is maintained for each participant, with all investment earnings accruing to him or her.

Because defined-contribution plans are, by definition, always fully funded, barring a failure to make the contribution, the obligation of the plan is fully discharged at all times. The level of retirement benefits depends on the return on the funds invested, which tends to increase with inflation. Therefore, defined-contribution plans can provide a partial hedge against inflation before and after retirement.

This Committee sees an important role for both defined-benefit and defined-contribution plans. We believe that each company should be free to choose the plan which suits it best and that public policy should be neutral on the subject. But there are certain regulatory requirements for defined-benefit programs under ERISA, such as restrictions involving prohibited transactions and reporting requirements, that should be streamlined and simplified where possible.

LEVEL OF COVERAGE

Given a continuation of the recent trend in participation in employer pensions, the vast majority of workers can look forward to receiving retirement benefits from private- or public-employer plans. Almost all large firms and unions already have some type of plan. The workers who are not covered by private plans tend to be nonunion employees of small and medium-size firms; employees in certain low-paying industries, in service trades and agriculture, and in newly established firms; or part-time and short-service workers. Even though ERISA has made it simpler to set up standardized plans, it is unlikely that any substantial number of these employers will establish new plans without changes in tax policy.

There is still a gap in private-sector pension coverage, and without the changes recommended in this policy statement, it will not readily be closed. **However, we do not agree with the suggestion that private pensions should be mandated by government for all employers.** Mandated private pensions would probably result in an inflexible pension system that would be inappropriate for many employers and their workers. Some employers who currently do not provide pension plans might be unable to pass the cost of such plans on to consumers and might therefore be forced out of business. Some of those who were able to establish private plans would attempt to reduce the costs of such pensions by reducing wages or restricting employment.

The government should develop incentives that will encourage employers to set up new plans on their own to meet the conditions of their particular industries. This could be accomplished in part by further simplifying ERISA, especially where small employers are concerned. **Another policy change to increase the coverage under employer plans would be to make all employee contributions to private plans from before-tax dollars and include any benefits received as part of taxable income. This change would go far toward encouraging greater use and adequacy of benefits of private pension plans.***

INFLATION

Inflation is the most serious and intractable economic problem facing retired and soon-to-be-retired employees. Their expenses go up, but their pension income usually does not keep pace. The problem has been brought into sharp focus recently by the largest persistent peacetime inflation in America's history.

Relief from inflationary erosion of retirement income will come in the long run only when effective overall government policies reestablish relatively stable price levels.[3]

Unfortunately, the government moved in an inflation-aggravating direction in the last decade in a number of areas, including its own retirement

---

[3]/ See *Fighting Inflation and Rebuilding a Sound Economy* (1980).

---

*See memorandum by JOHN F. WELCH, JR., page 63.

plans. Unconstrained by costs in the short run, the federal government has provided full and even excessive cost-of-living escalations for Social Security and for all federal-employee retirement systems, including military pensions. These escalations have been significantly larger than recent wage increases for the working population and are proving to be exceedingly costly. There is, in effect, a two-class system of retirement benefits, one based on the savings and investments of private and nonprofit employers and the other based on overly onerous tax revenue support for public employees. Such unequal treatment is already leading to serious questions concerning whether this high level of government pensions can and should continue to be supported by tax revenues.

Current inflation levels have also led some people to try to get the federal government to mandate the indexing of private-employer-plan benefits to inflation. **Such action would be exceedingly unwise because of its indeterminate cost burden for American industry, its intrusion by government into labor-management relations, and its aggravation of inflationary pressures.**

Most private pension plans do provide some protection against low or moderate rates of inflation, but these measures can never be sufficient to keep pace with the high rates of recent years.

Under most defined-benefit plans, some protection is afforded because retirement benefits are based on an average of final pay rates, which are themselves usually inflated. In addition, many employers make ad hoc increases in benefits for retired employees, but it is not realistic to expect that any significant protection against inflation can evolve from such efforts.

Some protection is also provided under defined-contribution plans if the pension funds are invested in a manner that provides a return more or less commensurate with the rate of inflation. Opportunities for such investment results flow from the tendency of interest rates and total returns on common stock to rise with inflation over the long run. Defined-contribution plans (including variable annuities) pass along all investment results to participants. This means that during periods of poor investment performance, such as the mid-1970s for common stocks, the benefits from such plans can even move in the opposite direction from the cost of living. But over longer periods, the investment results of defined-contribution plans have generally produced important increases in annuities paid.

There are several additional steps that employers can take in the short run to provide some relief. Some employers can, for example, give retired employees the choice between a defined-contribution and a defined-benefit plan. Some employers have offered alternatives that enhance future retirement benefits and thereby cushion the potential impact of inflation. A few corporations permit employees to have their initial retirement benefits reduced in exchange for a future percentage increase each year for life. Some companies allow employees to use savings in company-sponsored thrift plans to buy indexed supplements to their pension plans from insurance companies.

Two additional methods could achieve much greater acceptance if employee contributions to pension and savings plans were treated for income tax purposes like employer contributions, that is, if taxes were deferred until the contributions were received as benefits. This would encourage additional employee contributions to retirement plans, with many employers matching these amounts to supplement pension benefits. Employers who do not have savings plans might also wish to consider establishing such plans for employees, with contributions being at least partially matched by the employer. The accumulated amounts could be used by the employee at retirement to provide additional income as inflation protection.

The common theme of all such plans is that employees can protect themselves against inflation to some degree if they are willing to share the cost of that protection with their employer and if they recognize early enough their personal responsibility to save for retirement. But it is worth repeating that relief from inflationary erosion of retirement income will come in the long run only when sound government policies reestablish relatively stable price levels.

AGE OF RETIREMENT

By law, most employees must be permitted to remain on the job until age 70. Social Security still uses age 65 as the earliest age for full benefits, with early retirement available beginning at age 62 with reduced benefits. Employer retirement plans other than those in government generally use age 65 as their normal retirement age.

Many government-employer plans provide full benefits at early retirement ages. Federal civil service provides full benefits at age 55 with thirty years of service or at age 60 with twenty-five years of service. Military pensions provide full benefits after twenty years of service regardless of age. Workers in hazardous-duty occupations, such as police and fire fighters, also tend to use the twenty-year period without an age requirement. Early, nonreduced pension benefits are inordinately expensive and account for a very large part of the huge unfunded liability of government plans. The situation is exacerbated by the fact that federal civil service employees, most other federal workers, and some state and local government employees are not covered by Social Security and thus do not contribute to the overall social cost of the basic level of benefits.

Such generous early retirement full-benefit pensions may be justified for *some* employees in *specific* occupations, but much of the work in these occupations can be performed until normal retirement age. Restructuring the retirement age of these short-service full-benefit plans would be the most effective way to ensure the financial soundness of these specialized public-employer plans.

It is time for both employers and employees to reconsider their attitudes toward early retirement. Elimination of full-benefit or heavily subsidized retirement at early ages and gradual upward movement of normal retirement ages would help to reverse the current trend toward earlier retirement. Worries about the inroads made by inflation during long periods of retirement also seem to be giving workers second thoughts about early retirement. A shift toward later retirement would enable employer and employee contributions to employer pension plans to raise the general level of annual retirement income to be received at normal retirement ages. But employment patterns will also have to shift if the traditional retirement age rises. Just as the American economy has been able to accommodate, and benefit from, an enormous increase in the employment of women, it can also benefit from an increase in the employment of people over age 60 or even 65. This will require more flexible work assignments, including part-time, temporary, flexible-hour, and seasonal work arrangements and job sharing with younger part-time workers.

This Committee believes that employers and employees have widely varying needs and that they should be free to determine the retirement age at which full pension benefits will be paid, without government mandates.

But it also believes that government-employer plans have misused early retirement provisions at heavy expense to taxpayers, frequently deferring that expense to future generations of taxpayers. We believe early retirement under all public plans should generally be at actuarially reduced benefits.

Our 1978 policy statement *Jobs for the Hard-to-Employ: New Directions for a Public-Private Partnership* highlighted the benefits to both employers and employees of increasing training and job opportunities for mid-career and older workers as well as for retirees in ways that would make maximum use of these groups as a productive resource. In that statement, we urged employers to foster a smoother transition from regular work to retirement through such means as continuing education, skill renewal and retraining, reassignment of older workers, and part-time work and tapered retirement. We reaffirm that recommendation in this statement.

COVERING A MOBILE LABOR FORCE

A strong private-employer pension system is in the public interest; it encourages individuals to plan for their retirement and stimulates capital formation. However, optimal economic growth requires that capital and labor resources be relatively free to move to their most productive uses. This means that public policy should not encourage occupational, industrial, geographic, or other barriers to labor mobility.

A stable labor force encourages employers to invest in the on-the-job experience and training of their workers, but it is also important that pension policy should not unduly interfere with labor mobility. Because of increased international competitiveness and the need for greater technological change, the United States is entering a period during which economic change is likely to be even more rapid than it was in the past. Consequently, employers should design their pension plans not simply to meet the needs of the short term but to permit labor force adjustment to longer-term economic change.

VESTING

The term *vesting* refers to the rights that an employee acquires to a pension or a portion of a pension after completing a specified term of service. A vested employee has accrued pension rights whether or not he or she is working for the employer at retirement age. Unless major portions of an individual's working career lead to accrual and preservation of pension credits, employer retirement plans will not have a meaningful role to play in providing old-age security.

Before ERISA, plan sponsors had considerable discretion in setting service and age requirements for vesting, and many plans required an employee to spend his whole career with one employer in order to qualify for a pension. When ERISA was passed in 1974, however, employers were required to adopt some form of earlier vesting, with most opting for full vesting after ten years of service.

One argument for early vesting is that it allows more labor mobility. In a complex economy sensitive to technological advances and shifting market forces, the labor force needs to be fairly mobile, and employees need to be able to shift from one employer to another and from one sector of the economy to another.

Earlier vesting could expand the role of private pensions in the nation's retirement system. However, strong arguments against earlier vesting also exist in terms of anticipated higher costs, both in direct dollar outlays and in the possible earlier departure of experienced personnel. It is likely that any additional costs of earlier vesting would be passed along to present and future employees in the form of reduced wages, pensions, and other fringe benefits.

Recent actuarial studies show that under prevailing pension provisions, most employee turnover occurs within the first five years of employment. What is unknown is the extent to which earlier vesting would result in lowering turnover in the first five years of employment and in accelerating turnover after the five-year vesting requirement was satisfied.

We do not support a government mandate to reduce vesting requirements below their current levels. However, we do urge companies to consider the advantages of earlier vesting and to study possible employee reactions and the effects of earlier vesting on private pensions.*

A number of proposals have urged that the law require that a surviving spouse receive a portion of accrued vested pension benefits if an employee dies before early retirement. A divorced spouse would have the same entitlement on a prorated basis. Although we oppose mandating such benefits, we urge employers to consider establishing these rights voluntarily within their plans or through some other benefit arrangement such as a life insurance plan.

With respect to preretirement death benefits, we urge business to combine benefits from retirement plans and greater use of insurance to provide an adequate level of survivor benefits for families of workers who die. This would allow employers more flexibility in providing overall benefits.

PORTABILITY

Under ERISA, when a vested employee leaves one employer for another, his or her vested benefits can be left in the original plan or transferred to a successor plan with the consent of both plan sponsors, or the actuarial value of the benefits can be transferred to an IRA with the permission of the original sponsor.

Over the years, a great deal of attention has been given to the subject of portability, but not much of a positive nature has ensued. The important portability issue has to do with *vesting* and the *value* of the benefits vested.

Few problems exist under defined-contribution plans. Valuation of benefits for the departing employee is clear-cut; it is the accumulation in his or her account. Most such plans provide for continuing participation of the full accrued benefit amount in the original plan if an employee leaves before retirement. In addition, some allow the account balance to be transferred to an IRA, a life insurance company, or a new plan.

---

*See memoranda by THOMAS B. McCABE and by FRAZAR B. WILDE, page 65.

Collectively bargained multiemployer plans provide portability of benefits among participating employers. This works out well. However, accrued benefits can be lost if the participant leaves the jurisdiction of the multiemployer plan prior to meeting vesting requirements.

More complex problems arise with respect to vesting and portability of benefits in single-employer defined-benefit plans. One such problem has to do with the value of the benefits. If the funds are to be transferred to IRAs, life insurance company annuities, or a new-employer plan, should the full value be used even though the basic plan is underfunded? This is generally unfair to employees remaining in the original plan. Another problem has to do with "cold storage" vesting of benefits. The benefits vested when an employee leaves are almost always related to his or her final salary just before leaving; the original benefit is not escalated to reflect the ultimate final salary, as is true of persons who stay with the employer. Some have suggested that benefits of terminating employees should be adjusted by averaging up, but this would be difficult to administer and would impose an indeterminate cost on employer plans.

UNFUNDED LIABILITIES

The growing cost of pension programs has raised new concerns over what could become a potential problem: unfunded liabilities. Even though funding requirements were tightened under ERISA, there is always the risk that the failure of a major corporation could impose substantial costs through an increase in the premium rate that the Pension Benefit Guaranty Corporation would have to impose on other private-employer pension plans. In theory, a prosperous company should have no trouble meeting its obligations; but in fact, inflation is making it increasingly difficult to predict the resources needed to meet future benefit obligations. The problem is especially severe for multiemployer plans. Because a number of these plans are in economically troubled industries, there are fewer and fewer employers to share the pension load.

Under ERISA, the Pension Benefit Guaranty Corporation was established to insure private pensions. In the six years the corporation has been operating, the largest claim has been for $35 million. If the corporation, whose total assets hover around $250 million, were asked to take on a really large failure, it could be forced to levy a burdensome tax on the healthy funds that, by law, must support it.

In industries that have experienced prolonged adverse economic problems, such as some companies in the coal and automobile industries, there is concern about the impact of a failure of companies to meet their pension liabilities.

Most pension plans, when first installed, establish supplemental benefits to reflect service of employees prior to the introduction of the plan. These benefits are rarely fully funded immediately, but they tend to be funded over the first decades of the plans' existence.

Defined-contribution plans do not build up unfunded liabilities; current obligations to participants' benefit accounts are fully met each year. Defined-benefit plans providing career-average benefits also have no particular funding problems if adequate contributions are made currently.

For defined-benefit final-average-salary pension plans, however, the underfunding problem can be severe. Their degree of funding is affected by increased pension benefits reflecting an unexpected increase in final salaries, improved vesting, addition of survivor or disability benefits, and the extent to which actuarial assumptions fail to estimate future costs correctly. Of these causes, the largest and most difficult to deal with is unanticipated inflationary increases in final salary and therefore, automatically, in benefits reflecting all credited service.

The most seriously underfunded pension plans are to be found among federal plans. For example, the Civil Service Retirement System (CSRS) sets aside an amount equal to only 38 percent of payroll when 80 percent of payroll is necessary to fully fund the system. The military retirement plan is on a pay-as-you-go basis. Almost 100 percent of payroll would have to be set aside annually to actuarially fund the military plan. Current actuarial unfunded liabilities from these two plans exceed $750 billion, approximately 80 percent of the national debt.[4] Because they are not subject to standard pension regulations (such as ERISA), the public pensions have tended to be overly generous to current and future beneficiaries without taking into account the effect of this generosity on future taxpayers.

Business, labor, and the public have a strong stake in seeing that existing defined-benefit plans are well funded. The government and the Financial Accounting Standards Board have recently required private plans and plan sponsors to measure more accurately and report more fully on unfunded liabilities for accumulated benefits. The federal government should take action to apply the same reporting standards to public retirement plans. If this is done, it will become clear that benefits cannot be continually improved without commensurate increases in the level of funding.[5]

---

[4]/ President's Commission on Pension Policy, *Coming of Age: Toward a National Retirement Income Policy* (Washington, D.C.: U.S. Government Printing Office, February 25, 1981), pp. 18–19.

---

[5]/ For an additional approach to the underfunding problem, see discussion of book reserves in Chapter 5, pp. 57–58.

SOCIAL INVESTING

Most private pension assets are held, managed, and invested by banks, trust companies, investment advisors, and life insurance companies, although a growing proportion is being managed by the plan sponsors themselves. ERISA requires that plan assets be invested for the exclusive benefit of the plan participants and their beneficiaries. Prudent-man rules of fiduciary law also apply.

It is important to note that the vast majority of pension investments are "socially responsible" in that they provide jobs, housing, goods, services, buildings, and economic development, all of which benefit plan participants, society, and the economy. However, in recent years there have been calls for plan assets to be invested to achieve other objectives, even if such investments result in lower overall returns. Some would restrict investments in firms that are not unionized or that oppose unionization. Some urge more investment in low-income housing or health-care facilities. Others would deny pension assets to companies doing business in countries whose racial or political policies are in question.

We believe that the primary purpose of a pension plan investment is to provide the maximum return consistent with safety of principal for the benefit of its participants. We do not believe that there should be any additional government mandate with regard to the social or political direction of pension investments.

PUBLIC-EMPLOYER PENSION PLANS

Currently, there are 1.6 million former federal civil service employees receiving government pensions. The federal retirees generally receive pensions that are not only large by private-sector standards but also fully adjusted for the rising cost of living twice a year.[6] With double-digit inflation and the twice-a-year adjustment, the annual cost of the Civil Service Retirement System is substantial. In fiscal 1980, the annual cost of CSRS rose $1.3 billion as a result of the cost-of-living adjustment, bringing total outlays for 1980 to almost $15 billion. For fiscal 1981, it is estimated that the inflation adjustment will raise CSRS outlays to well over $17 billion.[7] Other federal government pensions, all of which are fully indexed for inflation, will also experience large increases in outlays in 1981.

---

[6] Beginning in fiscal 1982, the CSRS pension benefit will be indexed once a year.

[7] Dennis Klee Snook, "Cost of Living Adjustment in Civil Service Retirement," in Senate Budget Committee, *Indexation of Federal Programs* (Washington, D.C.: U.S. Government Printing Office, May 1981) p. 197.

Essentially, the CSRS benefits have been indexed to protect retirees against inflation since 1962. There have been a number of changes in the method of indexing, which for many years has meant that CSRS pension benefits have been fully indexed or overindexed. In contrast, it is estimated that between 3 and 7 percent of private pension plans are automatically adjusted for inflation, but almost all are capped at a maximum annual adjustment of 3 to 5 percent. About 10 percent of state and local public pension plans, covering 5 percent of all state and local employees, are adjusted annually without limit. About 45 percent of state and local pension plans are automatically adjusted with a cap similar to the cap used in the small proportion of private pensions that have automatic adjustments. [8]

Federal retirement plans cover less than 5 percent of the total U.S. civilian and military labor force and in 1980 paid over $25 billion to retirees. In contrast, private-employer pension plans paid only about the same amount in annual benefits to a substantially larger proportion of the labor force. The average pension benefit from the federal system (CSRS and military) is about two-and-a-half times higher than the average benefit from private plans. [9]

Even if allowance is made for a lower proportion of federal retirees receiving full career-related Social Security benefits, the cost of federal retirement plans is very high indeed. It would be much lower in total if federal employees were covered by Social Security and by a pension plan more typical of those in the private sector. [10]

Originally, the rationale for liberal public pensions was that government salaries were significantly lower than private-sector salaries. But since government salaries were made more comparable to those in the private sector, a process that began in 1962, no offsetting changes have been made in the generous pension formulas. **Any comparison of compensation for public- and private-sector employment should be made on the basis of total compensation, including benefits, not just salary.**

There are, in addition, some specific features of public pension plans that we believe policy makers should revise. (Some of these recommendations have been made earlier in this statement but are summarized here.)

---

[8] Snook, "Cost of Living Adjustment in Civil Service Retirement," *Indexation of Federal Programs,* p. 204.

---

[9] Based on data in President's Commission on Pension Policy, *Coming of Age: Toward a National Retirement Income Policy,* pp. 12-17.

---

[10] See Congressional Budget Office, Congress of the United States, *Options for Federal Civil Service Retirement: An Analysis of Costs and Benefit Provisions* (Washington, D.C.: U.S. Government Printing Office, 1978), pp. x-xi.

• **Early retirement.** Historically, early retirement was a means of compensating those in hazardous employment, first in the military and later in police and fire-fighting jobs. The concept has spread throughout most public systems, and it is now possible for all federal civil servants to retire with full benefits as early as age 55 if they have thirty years of service.[11] Government employees have exercised these generous early retirement options at considerable expense to the taxpayer. **We recommend that early retirement under all public plans should be at actuarially reduced benefits.**

• **Overlapping eligibility. We urge that all government workers be brought into the Social Security system and that government plans be carefully amended to protect all legitimate public service benefits.** As a compromise, if necessary, at least all new government employees should be brought into the system starting now. This change would eliminate what many perceive to be an inequity that allows government workers to meet the minimum eligibility requirements for collecting Social Security benefits earned in other jobs in addition to receiving very generous public pensions. The potential inequity arises because Social Security benefits are designed to be relatively generous to low-wage workers. The vast majority of government retirees currently collecting both Social Security benefits and a public-employer pension have had a relatively short history of work in the private sector and are therefore considered low-wage earners. As such, they receive the advantage of disproportionately high Social Security benefits, including full Medicare coverage.

• **Indexing.** The cumulative effect of twice-a-year indexing of public pensions to the CPI results in pensions that actually outstrip the real rate of inflation. We are opposed to full indexation of any employer pension benefits. **We urge Congress to reduce the indexing of public-employer retirement benefits to a portion of the CPI with an adjustment only once a year.** This would still provide public-employer pension benefits with a degree of protection against inflation, and such protection would still be substantially greater than the protection afforded private-sector retirees.

---

[11]/ Congressional Budget Office, *Options for Federal Civil Service Retirement: An Analysis of Costs and Benefit Provisions*, p. 8. Under special provisions for fire fighters and law enforcement officers, or in the case of a major agency cutback or some other type of involuntary separation, civil service employees may receive pensions before age 55.

- **Disability.** At the end of 1978, there were over 323,000 civil service retirees collecting disability benefits totaling about $2.2 billion a year. During that year, 32 percent of all new retirees retired on disability.[12] As many as 80 percent of uniformed workers in some local jurisdictions retire early on disability incomes. **Eligibility rules for disability benefits need to be tightened. Benefits should be included in taxable income, excess benefits should be eliminated, and cost-of-living adjustments should be reduced so that it does not pay workers who are only marginally disabled to remain on the disability rolls.**

At present, a civil service employee who is unable to do *one* central function of his or her job because of disease or disability is considered legally disabled. We believe that if a disabled employee can perform in other positions, the agency should have the authority to reassign or retrain that individual or require him or her to actively seek an alternative position or else lose the disability benefit.

---

[12] Philip K. Robins and Hoi S. Wai, "Disability Programs and Work Effort: Issues and Prospects," *Journal of the Insitute for Socioeconomic Studies* 6, no. 2 (Summer 1981): 55.

CHAPTER FIVE

TOWARD GREATER PERSONAL SAVING

The role of individual saving and investment is given insufficient attention as a source of income in retirement. As Social Security benefits have increased and as private pensions have grown, the traditional idea that an individual has both the need and the responsibility to set aside some portion of current income for old age has been emphasized less and less.

The United States has, in recent decades, had one of the lowest personal saving rates in the industrialized world. In 1973, personal savings as a proportion of personal disposable income were 7.8 percent; but by 1980, this share had declined to about 4 percent.[1]

Public policy has created an environment that discourages most people from relying on personal savings and investments as significant future sources of old-age economic support. A high and persistent rate of inflation has contributed to the decline in the rate of personal saving because individuals' expectations of continued higher prices reduce their incentive to save.

In addition, inflation and the existing tax structure have pushed all taxpayers into higher tax brackets. This has reduced the effective rate of return to individuals when their personal savings are in assets whose earnings are included in taxable income.

---

[1] Michael J. Boskin, Mark Gertler, and Charles Taylor, *The Impact of Inflation on U.S. Productivity and International Competitiveness* (Washington, D.C.: National Planning Association, 1980), p. 22.

The personal savings component of retirement income needs to increase. A higher level of personal saving and investment for retirement will give each individual maximum flexibility to adapt retirement income to his or her particular needs. In order for this goal to be achieved, however, there will have to be substantial changes in the general economic climate and in specific tax laws that now discourage saving.

Although inflation has depressed saving, there is also reason to believe that a low saving rate has served to aggravate inflation. Decreased saving rates have greatly reduced the capital available to modernize plant and equipment and to improve productivity and competitiveness. U.S. productivity growth has been slowing dramatically while demands on the economic system to meet the rapid expansion of social programs have been growing. A reversal in the current productivity trend will help in an anti-inflationary strategy, but this will require, among other things, a much higher rate of saving and investment.

Only a more productive economy can provide higher standards of living for people in *all* phases of their lives. We cannot stress too strongly that the success of all retirement programs, Social Security and employer pensions included, depends directly on the economy's ability to produce goods and services efficiently, competitively, and in greater amounts. To achieve this more productive economy, the country must begin to place more emphasis on investment and less on consumption. Critical to this shift will be increasing incentives *and* reducing disincentives for saving and investment in new and more productive plant and equipment.

RETIREMENT POLICIES AND CAPITAL FORMATION

The amount of money involved in both public- and private-sector employer retirement plans is so substantial that any effect these plans have on the level of saving is very significant. In general, funded private pensions are invested in the economy and thus contribute to capital formation. Recent studies have indicated that more than three-quarters of net personal savings come from savings through private-employer pension plans.

There is considerable concern that the Social Security system and its financing structure may have depressed personal saving and inhibited capital formation. In contrast with funded private pensions, the minimal reserves in the Social Security trust fund (and the reserves for federal pensions) are held in government securities rather than in private financial instruments. Consequently, even the very modest revenues generated from taxes under the pay-as-you-go Social Security system make no direct contribution to private capital formation.

In addition, some studies indicate that increases in the Social Security tax have a negative influence on the level of personal saving.[2] The expectation of a fairly large monthly Social Security payment that is fully indexed for inflation may encourage consumption and discourage saving by individuals prior to their retirement. This possible shift in the consumption-saving pattern is more likely in an inflationary period. (Fully indexed government pensions are likely to have a similar detrimental influence on saving.) Workers often regard Social Security payments as a "contribution" to the system, a sort of savings, even though all revenues are paid out almost immediately to current retirees.

Unfunded liabilities of public-employer plans are also becoming an increasingly significant claim on public resources. A substantial proportion of all public pensions are not advance-funded; consequently, as more and more of these employees reach retirement age, taxes must rise to cover the increased benefits. The cost of financing the expansion of benefits in such plans through higher taxes is likely to further dampen personal saving rates because it reduces disposable income. Even more damaging to increased saving and investment is a government policy which continually adopts fiscal policies that create deficits.

In contrast with Social Security and unfunded pension plans, funded private pensions are, in effect, an accumulation of employee and employer savings. As such, these plans are a strong prosaving force. Moreover, these funds are usually actively invested in the economy.

Several countries, including West Germany, Sweden, and Italy, have adopted approaches to corporate pension fund obligations that provide firms with an incentive to generate capital internally. Firms are permitted to recognize their full pension liability in any year as a book reserve on their balance sheet and take a tax deduction for a portion of the increase in the annual reserve. Although such an approach would have to be adapted to the situation in the United States, it could be used to partially satisfy funding requirements, particularly if the plan sponsor has other assets sufficient to cover 100 percent of the plan obligations to date. Obviously, in order to protect pension fund beneficiaries, the use of book reserves, even for some portion of the pension liability, would have to be limited in some way to those firms whose financial position is sound and those with some provision

---

[2]/ Certain other studies show a less significant or insignificant net effect of Social Security and pensions on personal saving. In the case of employer pensions, certain studies argue that their contribution to saving may be partially achieved through displacing savings in other forms. A key reason for this ambiguity with regard to the net effect of Social Security is that improvements in benefits can encourage earlier retirement, and many workers looking forward to more years of retirement living are thus motivated to build up their personal savings during their working years to help pay for those added nonworking years.

to protect the rights of beneficiaries in the event of plan failure. Nevertheless, because the book-reserve approach encourages employers with defined-benefit plans to recognize fully their plans' liabilities and to increase capital formation, it may be a constructive method of speeding up formal recognition of unfunded liabilities directly on the firms' balance sheets.

Other recommendations made elsewhere in this statement can also reduce disincentives and enhance incentives to saving. To be more specific, we believe that the recommendations made in Chapter 3 for changes in the indexation of Social Security benefits and a gradual increase in the retirement age will go a long way toward balancing the cost of Social Security with available resources and will eliminate the need for ever increasing tax and rate base hikes that could dampen the future growth of personal savings. In addition, our recommendations concerning employer pensions (Chapter 4) will broaden coverage and thereby add to the capital available for economic growth.

INCREASING SAVING

It is in society's interest to make increased individual savings for retirement a financially attractive and accessible goal. But changes in the tax law are necessary before a substantial number of current workers will be able and willing to increase their saving to any significant degree. **Tax proposals to encourage saving generally deserve favorable consideration because they will reduce the current consumption bias in the tax code and contribute to a higher level of investment.** Tax policies that directly encourage saving for retirement deserve the most emphasis of all. Accordingly, we give top priority in this area to the recommendation that persons covered by qualified pension plans be permitted to make tax-deferred contributions to either an IRA, a Keogh Plan, or to a qualified pension plan.

We recommend liberalizing the contribution limits for individual retirement plans such as Keogh Plans, IRAs, Limited Employee Retirement Accounts, and Simplified Pension Accounts. Upper contribution levels for these plans have varied, but all have been significantly below the level set for contributions to corporate plans. For example, prior to the enactment of the Economic Recovery Tax Act of 1981, contributions to IRAs, which have been used primarily by workers not covered by a corporate plan, were limited to $1,500 a year or 15 percent of income, whichever is less. Keogh Plans, used mostly by the self-employed, limit contributions to $7,500 or 15 percent of income, whichever is less. Under a defined-contribution corporate plan, ERISA permits a corporation to contribute to each individual's account as much as 25 percent of compensation up to $25,000 a year indexed to the CPI, which means that in 1981, the maximum contribution is 25 percent of compensation, or about $41,000 annually. In contrast, the limits set by ERISA for IRAs and Keoghs are not indexed.[3]

Liberalizing the limits of these types of retirement savings accounts will produce some tax deferment plus some initial tax loss for the federal government. How much will depend on the level of the new limits and the extent to which individuals utilize the accounts. In 1976, the initial revenue loss associated with IRAs was estimated to be $572 million. Persons with annual incomes over $50,000 accounted for about 8 percent of IRA participants and about 20 percent of the revenue loss. This, of course, means that over 90 percent of the participants, accounting for 80 percent of the initial revenue loss, had annual incomes of less than $50,000. Indeed, a comparison of 1976 and 1977 tax returns shows that although the rate of utilization of IRAs among high-income earners increased, a small but increasing proportion of those with low incomes (less than $15,000 adjusted gross income) also utilized IRAs.[4]

There is every reason to believe that a liberalization of the contribution limits of these kinds of retirement accounts will produce a significant increase in their use by individuals in all income groups. This was the experience in Canada when limits for IRA-type programs were expanded. Although it is recognized that such a tax policy change may cause some modest displacement of other forms of savings (including increased borrowing to take advantage of new contribution limits on these accounts), we believe the additional net savings will be substantial.

The magnitude of the increase in savings is likely to be especially high when accompanied by across-the-board personal tax rate reductions that increase disposable income. Such individual retirement plans have the great advantage of practically locking in the increased saving for use in capital formation because of the low incidence of preretirement withdrawal of such funds. This low withdrawal rate is partly due to the tax disadvantage of withdrawal during an individual's high earning years. The relatively stable base of investable funds, in turn, allows the institution managing the funds to invest them in the kind of longer-term securities typically used by firms and individuals to finance private capital formation.

---

[3] The tax treatment of defined-benefit plans is also much more favorable than the tax treatment of IRAs and Keoghs. Defined-benefit plans can pay benefits up to 100 percent of the average of the highest three years' salary up to the limit of approximately $111,000 annually in 1980.

---

[4] Ray Schmitt, "Pensions and Indexation: An Analysis of the Effect of Inflation on Retirement Income," in Senate Budget Committee, *Indexation of Federal Programs* (Washington, D.C.: U.S. Government Printing Office, May 1981), p. 400.

Encouraging individual saving for retirement has another advantage, that of serving as a more powerful force for attracting the increase in discretionary income produced by tax cuts into savings and productivity-enhancing investments. This is especially important if the current unacceptably high rate of inflation is to be reduced.

Specifically, we recommend:

● The current maximum annual tax-deductible contributions permitted under personal retirement plans (such as Keogh Plans and IRAs) should be raised substantially.

● The eligibility rules for IRAs should be liberalized so that even those individuals already covered by a private-employer plan can establish a supplemental retirement account on their own up to an appropriate limit.

● The upper limit for the combined total of tax-deductible annual contributions to all such individual and defined-contribution corporate retirement plans on behalf of any one individual should move much closer to the annual maximum of about $41,000 currently allowed for a person under a defined-contribution corporate pension plan.

● Businesses that already provide pension plans for their employees should consider integrating some measure of individual saving into benefit packages through such mechanisms as matching thrift programs, profit sharing, and voluntary employee contributions.

We recognize that these liberalized limits should be phased in gradually in order to take into account the extent of saver response and to keep their effect on federal tax revenues consistent with maintaining an appropriate degree of overall budget discipline. **As a first step, the limits on these types of accounts could be immediately set at levels as if indexed under ERISA in the same way the maximum limit under defined-contribution corporate plans is indexed.** For 1980, this would have raised the IRA limit from $1,500 to $2,213 and the Keogh limit from $7,500 to $11,063.

It is also important to continue to adjust these maximum contribution limits automatically. Without such adjustments, the gap between the maximum limit under defined-contribution corporate plans and the IRA and Keogh maximum limits will widen in the future. Policy makers should apply an automatic adjustment to the IRA and Keogh maximum limits once the gradual process of raising the limits to a level more comparable to the maximum level for defined-contribution plans has been achieved.[5]

---

[5]/ Note that this type of indexing has an anti-inflationary rather than a proinflationary bias because it encourages more saving the higher prices rise.

CED has pointed out that policy makers traditionally have overestimated the importance of the resulting initial revenue loss and undervalued the later tax revenues the Treasury will receive. As we have urged in our tax recommendation for more rapid capital recovery to stimulate investment in plant and equipment (see *Stimulating Technological Progress*, 1980), the initial revenue loss from tax reductions should take into account the dynamic feedback to tax revenues that greater saving, investment, and output will produce.

The enactment of the Economic Recovery Tax Act of 1981 includes a number of tax incentives to encourage saving for retirement. These incentives include raising the annual maximum contribution to IRAs and Keogh Plans and permitting active participants in employer-sponsored plans to establish IRAs.[6] Because these policy changes are precisely in the direction recommended by this Committee, we strongly endorse them. If, as we expect, experience shows that these incentives produce significant net savings, we recommend that policy makers consider additional incentives to bring the maximum annual contribution levels under IRAs and Keoghs even closer to the level currently permitted for defined contributions to corporate plans. We also look forward to the implementation of the other recommendations in this statement that further strengthen both the private-employer pension and the individual savings components of retirement policy because these are also critically important both to retirees and to future economic growth.

---

[6] The following tax policy changes affecting retirement income will become effective in January 1982: The maximum contribution to an IRA will be increased from $1,500 to the lesser of $2,000 or 100 percent of an individual's earnings for the year. Individuals who are active participants in an employer-sponsored retirement plan will be able to deduct up to $2,000 a year of contributions to IRAs. Voluntary contributions to employer-sponsored plans will also qualify. The maximum deductible contribution to a Keogh Plan will be increased from $7,500 to $15,000.

62

MEMORANDA OF COMMENT, RESERVATION, OR DISSENT

Pages 6, 12, and 15, by ROBERT R. NATHAN with which BRUCE K. MacLAURY and THOMAS J. EYERMAN have asked to be associated

In this policy statement, emphasis is repeatedly placed on the need to increase savings and investment and to regard this objective as an important factor in determining retirement policies. It is of major importance to step up our pace of capital formation in order to modernize our plant and equipment, to help improve productivity, and to strengthen the competitive capability of American industry in the increasingly internationalized business environment.

But the conclusion that our essential purpose should be to increase the level of savings, as a specific objective, is debatable. Unless there is a much higher effective demand for plant and equipment outlays, efforts focused on stepping up the pace of personal savings could lead to relatively lower levels of consumer expenditures and higher government deficits. The policy goals should be designed directly to encourage more investment in plant and equipment. An increase in private investment will most likely bring forth the essential level of savings to finance capital formation at much higher levels. A substantial reduction in federal deficits would occur if the economy is invigorated by higher levels of investment, and that would make more funds available for funding private capital formation.

The general goals of funding the private pension systems and encouraging individuals to save for their retirement years are certainly desirable from the pension and retirement point of view. However, the constant repetition on the important contribution that pension policy can make to increased savings and investment lends little credence to the otherwise high quality of this policy statement.

Page 8, by J. W. McSWINEY

Removing inducements for older employees to choose early retirement can cause a significant slowdown in career paths for younger and mid-career persons.

Pages 8 and 37, by RAPHAEL CARRION, JR.

I realize that changing the retirement age from age 65 to age 68 is something that has to be phased in gradually. Extending it to the year 2000 seems to be much too slow, and by that time, retirement at age 68 will probably be as obsolete as age 65 seems now. I would, therefore, prefer to see a faster phasing-in of retirement at age 68 and a built-in formula that would regularly extend the retirement age in line with life expectancy.

Pages 9, 31, and 43, by JOHN F. WELCH, JR.

I cannot endorse the recommendation that tax treatment of Social Security be reversed for a number of reasons:

1. The change would present a complex problem of administration to ensure equity to those who have contributed to Social Security from aftertax dollars. Their Social Security retirement income would have to be taxed at a different rate from other income.
2. A sizable loss of general revenues would be incurred without any improvement to the Social Security funding problem.
3. Reducing the net cost of employee contributions could pave the way for comparable increases in the tax. This would be tantamount to financing Social Security from general revenues.
4. Finally, given the history of tax-free Social Security benefits and a current climate which casts doubts on the viability of the system, the recommendation to tax Social Security benefits is untimely.

Page 9, by ROBERT R. NATHAN

For funding some parts of the Social Security system, general revenue financing should not be ruled out. At a time when income taxes are being cut drastically, as evidenced by the reduction of ceiling marginal rates on all income taxes from 70 percent to 50 percent, there is need for careful reappraisal of total financing of all Social Security benefits by the regressive payroll tax.

There is no major tax more burdensome on the middle- and lower-income groups than the payroll tax. Some of the figures included in this statement indicating possible doubling of the rates of payroll taxation in the next half century should give pause to those who fully understand the incidence of the payroll tax. Rather than repeatedly reducing the progressive income tax and increasing the regressive payroll tax, consideration ought to be given to financing such components of the Social Security system as Medicare and disability benefits from general revenues.

The Social Security system is not strictly actuarial. While it is important to relate benefits to earnings levels and to retain a connection between payroll taxes and benefits, rigid resistance to the use of general revenue financing for some Social Security benefits will result in increasingly heavy burdens on the middle- and low-income recipients relative to the higher-income levels. This could lead in time to a major rather than moderate shift to general revenue financing.

Pages 9 and 38, by JOHN H. FILER with which THOMAS J. EYERMAN and HAROLD M. WILLIAMS have asked to be associated

In the long run, the national interest will indeed be best served by a properly structured and universal Social Security system. However, I do not believe it appropriate to call for the mandatory extension of the system, even to new workers, at this time. I do believe that the goal of universal coverage will be more easily achieved if those now outside the system are presented with a well-functioning, properly structured system. The problems in the system, as evidenced by both the current financial problem and by projection of tax rates in the future, need undivided attention now.

Public awareness of the problems in the Social Security system provides lawmakers with a unique opportunity to eliminate many of the major flaws in the system. The difficulties in availing of this opportunity will be great. There is considerable and very effective opposition to any change in the system, especially an increase in the retirement age. To divert energies to trying for mandatory extension of the system would be counterproductive. Furthermore, the constitutional issues involved in mandatory coverage of employees of state and local governments could well present an insurmountable legal obstacle to extension. In any event, these constitutional issues, which have not been addressed in this report, would lead to protracted litigation if coverage were mandated. There is also a risk that, if successful, mandatory extension would reduce the feeling of urgency about fixing the system. Inclusion of a new group of active workers without a corresponding increase in current beneficiaries would increase income but not expenditures. This infusion of cash would have short-term benefits but would have minimal long-term effect, reducing projected tax rates only marginally.

The problem of inequitably large benefits, so-called windfall benefits, for those government workers who accumulate minimal Social Security coverage does need to be addressed. I urge that efforts be made to develop a fair and easily understood mechanism for elimination of this flaw.

Page 10, by THOMAS B. McCABE

The limit of $500 on a lump-sum cash withdrawal from a pension plan is too small.

Page 10, by J. W. McSWINEY

Any variation of portable pensions will involve administrative complexities that probably will rule out voluntary acceptance by employers.

Page 11, by FRAZAR B. WILDE

I agree that matching thrift plans can be used as vehicles for integrating some measure of individual savings into their benefit programs. To be successful, they must provide the same tax advantages as profit-sharing plans, which is not the case under the 1981 tax law.

Page 12, by JOHN SAGAN

Care must be exercised on the part of government in establishing regulations and guidelines and on the part of pension providers in providing pension plans to ensure that capital formation and savings should be encouraged in our diverse and free economy. It is, of course, the role of the government and of providers to ensure that proper safeguards for employee rights are taken.

Page 31, by THOMAS B. McCABE

The fundamental reason for the earnings test was to assure that Social Security recipients actually left the work force in order to provide jobs for younger workers. Social Security was enacted in a depression environment.

Page 35, by ROBERT A. BECK with which JOHN SAGAN has asked to be associated

Serious consideration should also be given to use of the Personal Consumption Expenditure (PCE) deflator to measure increases in the cost of living. The PCE deflator avoids two major problems inherent in the Consumer Price Index (CPI). The PCE deflator treats housing costs more appropriately and is based on an up-to-date market basket. During the 1970s, price increases as measured by the CPI rose by approximately 1 percent more per year than the price increases as measured by the chain-weighted PCE deflator. During 1979 and 1980, the CPI-measured increases exceeded those measured by the PCE deflator by 3.0 percent and 2.1 percent, respectively.

Page 48, by THOMAS B. McCABE

Vesting of fewer than ten years of service usually results in an insignificant retirement benefit, considering that a terminated vested worker with fewer than ten years of service may be twenty-five to thirty years away from collecting his vested benefit and inflation is eroding it during all those years.

Page 48, by FRAZAR B. WILDE

The statement urging companies to consider the advantages of earlier vesting is impractical. If it is a reasonable goal, it will require more than a mild suggestion, particularly in this era of rising benefit costs.

OBJECTIVES OF THE COMMITTEE FOR ECONOMIC DEVELOPMENT

For thirty-five years, the Committee for Economic Development has been a respected influence on the formation of business and public policy. CED is devoted to these two objectives:

To develop, through objective research and informed discussion, findings and recommendations for private and public policy which will contribute to preserving and strengthening our free society, achieving steady economic growth at high employment and reasonably stable prices, increasing productivity and living standards, providing greater and more equal opportunity for every citizen, and improving the quality of life for all.

To bring about increasing understanding by present and future leaders in business, government, and education and among concerned citizens of the importance of these objectives and the ways in which they can be achieved.

CED's work is supported strictly by private voluntary contributions from business and industry, foundations, and individuals. It is independent, nonprofit, nonpartisan, and nonpolitical.

The two hundred trustees, who generally are presidents or board chairmen of corporations and presidents of universities, are chosen for their individual capacities rather than as representatives of any particular interests. By working with scholars, they unite business judgment and experience with scholarship in analyzing the issues and developing recommendations to resolve the economic problems that constantly arise in a dynamic and democratic society.

Through this business-academic partnership, CED endeavors to develop policy statements and other research materials that commend themselves as guides to public and business policy; for use as texts in college economics and political science courses and in management training courses; for consideration and discussion by newspaper and magazine editors, columnists, and commentators; and for distribution abroad to promote better understanding of the American economic system.

CED believes that by enabling businessmen to demonstrate constructively their concern for the general welfare, it is helping business to earn and maintain the national and community respect essential to the successful functioning of the free enterprise capitalist system.

STATEMENTS ON NATIONAL POLICY
ISSUED BY THE RESEARCH AND POLICY COMMITTEE

*Statements issued in association with CED counterpart organizations in foreign countries.

CED COUNTERPART ORGANIZATIONS IN FOREIGN COUNTRIES

Close relations exist between the Committee for Economic Development and independent, nonpolitical research organizations in other countries. Such counterpart groups are composed of business executives and scholars and have objectives similar to those of CED, which they pursue by similarly objective methods. CED cooperates with these organizations on research and study projects of common interest to the various countries concerned. This program has resulted in a number of joint policy statements involving such international matters as energy, East-West trade, assistance to the developing countries, and the reduction of nontariff barriers to trade.

CE	Círculo de Empresarios *Serrano Jover 5-2°, Madrid 8, Spain*
CEDA	Committee for Economic Development of Australia *139 Macquarie Street, Sydney 2001,* *New South Wales, Australia*
CEPES	Europäische Vereinigung für Wirtschaftliche und Soziale Entwicklung *Reuterweg 14,6000 Frankfurt/Main, West Germany*
IDEP	Institut de l'Entreprise *6, rue Clément-Marot, 75008 Paris, France*
経済同友会	Keizai Doyukai (Japan Committee for Economic Development) *Japan Industrial Club Bldg.* *1 Marunouchi, Chiyoda-ku, Tokyo, Japan*
PSI	Policy Studies Institute *1-2 Castle Lane, London SW1E 6DR, England*
SNS	Studieförbundet Näringsliv och Samhälle *Sköldungagatan 2, 11427 Stockholm, Sweden*